AF686029

November 2010

Michael-

Thank you for recognizing the importance of electing fairminded secretaries of State! On to the next round.

Warmly,

Jocelyn

STATE SECRETARIES OF STATE

Election Law, Politics, and Theory

Series Editor: David Schultz

Election Law, Politics, and Theory broadly examines election law at the national, subnational, and international or comparative levels. Titles in the series provide both empirical and theoretical analysis of topics and issues that affect voting, campaigns, and elections, and as such offer coverage of political as well as legal concerns and controversies. Useful for scholars, researchers, and practitioners in the field, volumes address such subjects as voting rights, reapportionment, ballot access, campaign finance reform, the courts and election regulation, and the role of actors including political parties and the media. The series' ultimate goal is to build scholarship in this key area by seeking to understand how elections function in an increasingly complex, technological, and global community, and the ways in which election law impacts outcomes, disputes, and eventually governance in particular nations and societies.

State Secretaries of State

Guardians of the Democratic Process

JOCELYN F. BENSON
Wayne State University Law School, USA

ASHGATE

Published by
Ashgate Publishing Limited
Wey Court East
Union Road
Farnham
Surrey, GU9 7PT
England

Ashgate Publishing Company
Suite 420
101 Cherry Street
Burlington
VT 05401-4405
USA

www.ashgate.com

British Library Cataloguing in Publication Data
Benson, Jocelyn F.
State secretaries of state : guardians of the democratic process. -- (Election law, politics, and theory)
1. Cabinet officers--United States. 2. Elections--United States.
I. Title II. Series
352.2'93'0973-dc22

Library of Congress Cataloging-in-Publication Data
Benson, Jocelyn F.
State secretaries of state : guardians of the democratic process / by Jocelyn F. Benson.
p. cm. -- (Election law, politics, and theory)
Includes bibliographical references and index.
ISBN 978-0-7546-7745-1 (hardback) -- ISBN 978-0-7546-9482-3 (ebook) 1. Election law--United States--States. 2. Secretaries of State (State governments)--United States. I. Title.
KF4886.B46 2010
342.73'07--dc22

2009040126

ISBN 9780754677451 (hbk)
ISBN 9780754694823 (ebk)

Mixed Sources
Product group from well-managed forests and other controlled sources
www.fsc.org Cert no. SA-COC-1565
© 1996 Forest Stewardship Council
FSC

Printed and bound in Great Britain by
MPG Books Group, UK

Contents

This book is dedicated to all of the men and women who have worked since the founding of our country to make the American system of democracy open and accessible to all.

Foreword

Mark Ritchie, Secretary of State, Minnesota

Secretaries of State perform a wide range of public services—from business services and securities regulations to historical and cultural heritage promotion and of course, elections. One thing at the core of most of this work is the task of certifying official acts relating to government—including public documents, official signatures, enacted legislation, emergency declarations, and final election results.

This role, certifying the veracity or legitimacy of official actions, goes back to the Middle Ages when this function was performed largely by church officials. By the time of our Revolutionary War, Charles Thomson, the Secretary of the Continental Congress, had raised the profile of this certification task to one that the British Monarchy considered treasonous and subject to hanging. Undeterred by British threats, Secretary Thomson kept the official records and publicly "attested" to the veracity of all documents signed by President John Hancock, including the Declaration of Independence.

This task of independently certifying the accuracy and truthfulness of official documents and reports is the underlying logic for Secretaries of State being assigned the title of Chief Elections Officer in most states and being responsible for the final certification of results. With this authority comes a great responsibility. To be the certifier of truth and accuracy is to demand a very different standard for ourselves than is commonly assumed among politicians. From the earliest recorded history of election campaigns there has been a tendency for candidates and their supporters to stretch or bend the truth, especially when it comes to the views or actions of their perceived political opponents. This has been especially vicious inside modern political parties, where endorsement and primary election battles have become extreme at times.

Secretaries of State special responsibility has been highlighted over the past few election cycles, as close races have turned into highly visible recounts in Washington State, Virginia, New York, Minnesota, and of course Florida. While Florida has been the most high profile, it is also the only one that has been truly controversial. The care taken by Secretary Sam Reed in Washington State in the extremely close Governor's race in 2004 is a legend among other Secretaries who have faced, or fear they will face, similar situations.

This book provides an opportunity to hear about some of the finest public servants in the nation—Secretaries of State who come from many different political backgrounds and affiliations but who bring a nonpartisan, "public-trust first" perspective and approach to all the different tasks that they face, including elections. Readers who are as captivated by these stories may just become so motivated that they decide to run for Secretary of State themselves. That would make me, and I am guessing most other Secretaries, extremely happy and proud.

Mark Ritchie
Secretary of State, Minnesota
May 19, 2009

Preface

It is a tremendous honor to have the opportunity to write a book that details the crucial role that state Secretaries of State and other statewide election administrators play in promoting and protecting the American democratic process. For if elections are the bedrock of our American democracy, a state's chief election official is our mason.

In recent years, we as a nation witnessed the increasingly prominent role of Secretaries of State in recent elections, beginning in 2000 with the role of Florida Secretary Katherine Harris. Secretary Harris ran the Florida election in 2000 and oversaw the recount of the closest presidential election in our country's history. And, as a co-chair of Bush's Florida campaign who flew to New Hampshire to campaign for him during the primaries, Harris was widely presumed to have based her decisions on the advice of then-Governor Bush's national campaign strategists.

But 2000 was just the beginning of our modern obsession with election administration. In 2002, Congress passed the Help America Vote Act, paving the way for the purchase of millions of new electronic voting machines. The machines were subsequently decertified in several states after Secretaries found them to be easily subject to tampering. Then in 2004, Ohio Secretary Ken Blackwell endured controversy as he made several contentious decisions as Ohio's chief elections official and subsequently took credit for helping deliver the state of Ohio to President Bush's re-election. Two years later, at the American Democracy Conference in Washington DC following the 2006 election, then FEC Chairman Michael Toner said "The state of election administration in this country has been an embarrassment."

This book seeks to expand the story beyond the controversial headlines of a few Secretaries. While emphasizing what the Harris/Blackwell controversies underscored, the unparalleled role of a state's chief elections official in overseeing a smooth election, the following chapters illustrate the honorable, creative, innovative, and far reaching work that Secretaries of State have engaged in over the same decade that the negative stories captured headlines. The stories and case studies reinforce the central role of a state election administrator in promoting a healthy democracy, and highlight the work that Secretaries from all walks of life are doing to serve as guardians of the election process.

Who is the State Secretary of State?

All entities that play a role in the electoral process have a responsibility of promoting a healthy democracy, one free from discrimination, political pressures, and enabling the participation of the informed voter.[1] But it is the state Secretary of State who consistently serves at the "front lines" before, during, and after an election, and who is positioned as a bridge between the policy making entities—Congress, state legislatures—and the election officials who implement those policies. As such, it is the state Secretary of State who is most responsible for developing and executing policies and programs that further the dual interests at the core of democracy: ensuring accurate electoral outcomes, including efforts to reduce fraud or intimidation and promote integrity, and prioritizing access to the vote to enable the full, uniform, and equal participation of the electorate in the democratic process.[2]

In thirty-seven states, the state Secretary of State is the chief administrator of all elections. In all but seven of those thirty-seven states the Secretary of State is elected by the voters in a popular election. Legislatures elect their state's Secretaries in Tennessee, Maine and New Hampshire, and Governors appoint Secretaries in Florida, New Jersey, Pennsylvania, and Texas. In ten states—Illinois, South Carolina, Virginia, Wisconsin, New York, Maryland, Hawaii, Delaware, North Carolina, Oklahoma—the statewide oversight of election administration is in the hands of appointed boards or committees, comprised of as few as three (Oklahoma), or as many as twelve (Wisconsin) appointed members. In Utah, Hawaii, and Alaska, the Lieutenant Governor oversees election administration for the state.

Of course, a state's chief election official or board is a direct extension of the government, and thus they may only engage in actions that they are permitted to take under state law. For example, Secretary of State of California Debra Bowen was specifically empowered under California law to "conduct periodic reviews of voting systems to determine if they are defective, obsolete, or otherwise unacceptable."[3]

---

1 Raleigh Levine, *The (Un)Informed Electorate: Insights into the Supreme Court's Electoral Speech Cases*, 54 Case W. Res. L. Rev. 225 (2004).

2 Several commentators have also noted the partisan undertone to the access/accuracy divide, see, e.g., 73 Geo. Wash. L. Rev. 1206 at 1233 (describing "HAVA's access/integrity compromise"). See also Richard L. Hasen, *Beyond the Margin of Litigation: Reforming US Election Administration to Avoid Electoral Meltdown*, 62 Wash. & Lee L. R. 937 (2005) at 983–85 (proposing a model for nonpartisan election administration "where the allegiance ... is to the integrity of the process itself, and not to any particular electoral outcome"). It is just as important for a Secretary of State to bridge this partisan divide and recognize a balanced approach that administers elections in a way that furthers both goals.

3 California Elections Code section 19222.

But whether an official has wide or cabined discretion within the boundaries of state law, her ability to exercise judgment and influence over how elections are administered is significant.[4] To that end, the Secretary of State[5] is not simply charged with running elections, but is responsible for administering them in such a way that effectively promotes two values that are at the heart of a healthy democratic process: integrity and access.[6] It is particularly crucial for a Secretary to be mindful of this balance because some policies that are designed to promote integrity, such as voter identification requirements, can lead to the formation of barriers to voting and participation.[7] But with careful administration, such effects may be offset by corresponding policies that ease or alter registration requirements, or enable citizens to vote early in the days preceding the official Election Day.

Research for this Book

The research for this book was conducted over several months in 2008, during a sabbatical from my position as Assistant Professor of Law at Wayne State University Law School. In addition to reviewing various primary and secondary resources describing the work of current and former Secretaries, collected with the help of my Research Assistants Peter Sauer and Lena Kemal, I spent several hours meeting with thirty of the thirty-seven sitting Secretaries of State who oversee elections in their state.

The accessibility of many of these Secretaries was striking. South Dakota Secretary of State Chris Nelson answered the phone directly and scheduled his own interview. Minnesota Secretary of State Mark Ritchie responded to email requests within minutes. At the other end of the spectrum, scheduling time to meet with

4 Several commentators have suggested confining a Secretary of State's discretion, but admit that it is impossible to completely eliminate it. See, e.g., Hasen, *supra* note 2 at 978–79; *Note: Toward a Greater State Role in Election Administration*, 118 Harv. L. Rev. 2314 at 2315–16 (2005) (discussing proposals for "precisely designed rules—like crafting a precise definition for what constitutes a valid vote" for state election administrators).

5 Because the Secretary of State is the chief election administrator in thirty-seven of fifty states, with appointed boards of elections or Lieutenant Governor charged with this responsibility in thirteen other states, this article will use the term "Secretary of State" to refer to the entity in the state that is primarily responsible for overseeing the administration of elections in the state.

6 See 42 U.S.C. 1973gg(b) NVRA, stating that the purpose of promoting the exercise of the right to vote, a duty held by "Federal, State, and Local Governments," involved both "establish[ing] procedures that will increase the number of eligible citizens who register to vote in elections for Federal office" as well as "protect[ing] the integrity of the electoral process; and … ensur[ing] that accurate and current voter registration rolls are maintained."

7 Spencer Overton, *Voter Identification*, 105 Mich. L. Rev. 631, 634–35 (2007) (discussing the lack of evidence of widespread voter fraud, and its justification for voter identification requirements).

some Secretaries was not always as easy—many required detailed applications and descriptions of the project before agreeing to be interviewed, some scheduled interviews that were subsequently cancelled and never rescheduled, and some simply ignored my requests to meet.

While many were understandably hesitant to participate initially, perhaps due to the fact that most interviews were conducted in the months leading up to the 2008 presidential election, I greatly appreciated the time each Secretary gave to share their wisdom and experiences in support of this project. I am particularly thankful to have had the opportunity to meet with Indiana Secretary of State Todd Rokita and other Secretaries who may have been initially wary of whether this book would ultimately provide a fair and intellectually honest description of their work. I hope that the finished product within these chapters is an accurate and balanced summary of the many honorable projects in which so many Secretaries are engaged.

In the time I spent conducting interviews for this book, there were many unique and memorable moments. I spoke with Alabama Secretary of State Beth Chapman on her cell phone as she was en route to certify the results for the November 2008 elections. I discussed with Georgia Secretary of State Karen Handel, whose intelligence is rivaled only by her warmth, the minute details of her efforts to educate Georgia voters of the state's voter identification requirement. I met with Maine Secretary of State Matt Dunlap, who was extremely down to earth, unscripted, and candid, in a former one-room school house that is now his office in Augusta, Maine. And I benefited from the accessibility of Secretary of State Mark Ritchie, who never failed to quickly and directly respond to an email seeking information. I owe a great deal of thanks to him for his early enthusiastic encouragement and sincere support of this project.

I am also thankful to the Secretaries who were willing to take time out of their busy schedules to meet with me in person while they attended the July 2008 Summer Convention of the National Association of Secretaries of State (NASS), held in my home state of Michigan and sponsored by the Michigan Department of State. Current NASS President and Pennsylvania Secretary of State Pedro Cortés was particularly accommodating, meeting with me twice on the day he was sworn in as President of the Association.

But the aspect of my research that was the most rewarding, enlightening, informative, and inspiring were the two days I spent in Concord, New Hampshire with Secretary of State Bill Gardner. Gardner is currently the longest serving Secretary of State and the "Dean" of the collective Secretaries. I flew out to New Hampshire to meet with him, at the urging of several of his colleagues, and learned more in the hours I spent meeting with him in his State Capitol office than most political history majors do in an entire collegiate career. One of Gardner's favorite quotes is from Oliver Wendell Holmes—"An ounce of history is worth a pound of logic." Gardner's presence as a sitting Secretary, his dedication to fair elections, and his willingness to share his own experiences with anyone willing to listen, including many current Secretaries whom he mentors, ensures that the history he has witnessed in his thirty-plus years as Secretary will inform the work of those administering democracy in many years to come.

I also wish to thank the many individuals who assisted with the progress of this book throughout the course of its development. Put simply, this book would not have come to fruition were it not for the generous support of the Cohn family, who through former Wayne State University Law School Dean Frank Wu appointed me as the Cohn family endowed scholar in the fall of 2008. Being named as the Cohn scholar, and the subsequent financial support, enabled me to thoroughly research and develop this book. I am extremely grateful to the Cohn family for providing such support.

This book would also not exist without the efficient and tireless work of my research assistants, particularly Lena Kemal and Peter Sauer, who worked at all hours to help me schedule and transcribe my interviews with Secretaries while researching and verifying all background information. I am also grateful to Matt Cameron for assisting with the development of the individual profiles for each Secretary, along with Shamyle Nesfield, Stephanie Copabianco, Nicole Adams, Erin Bartos, and Lauren Leto for their additional research assistance.

Overview of the Chapters

It is my hope that this book provides a readable and informative description of the various roles that a state's Secretary of State (or any state's chief election administrator) is able to play when it comes to administering elections. The chapters seek to detail several different areas of election law and administration where the Secretary of State plays a crucial, if not pivotal, role in ensuring their state's democratic system is accessible and accurate. The first three chapters seek to emphasize the preeminent role of the modern state Secretary of State in promoting democracy while detailing the relations between Secretaries and the two entities that exert perhaps the most influence over their work: Congress and Political Parties. While Chapter 1 specifically describes the contemporaneous roles that Congress, the U.S. Justice Department, state and federal courts, and state legislatures play in election administration, Chapter 2 explores the tension between the need for Secretaries to serve as nonpartisan overseers of the political process and any loyalty or obligation they may feel to the political party that enabled their rise to the position. Similarly, Chapter 3 examines the impact of congressional oversight of elections on the ability of Secretaries to exercise their own independent authority to promote democracy, specifically describing the impact of three pieces of federal legislation—the Voting Rights Act of 1965, the National Voter Registration Act of 1993, and the Help America Vote Act of 2002—on the work of Secretaries of State.

The remaining chapters detail the various roles that Secretaries with election oversight authority play on a regular basis. Chapters 4, 5, and 6 examine the Secretaries in their role as the state's chief advocate for voters, primary educator for voting, and champion of election reforms. Chapter 7 details the importance of the Secretary in promoting access to voting for citizens with special needs, including English Learning and LEP voters, voters with physical disabilities, voters living overseas, or voters serving in the military. And Chapters 8, 9, and 10 detail the unique legal role of the Secretary in protecting the integrity of the elections process, enforcing all relevant campaign finance and election laws, and certifying signatures or the results of elections, including overseeing recounts. In addition, between each chapter is a short profile on a recent Secretary of State. The profiles seek to highlight some of the many Secretaries who go above and beyond their statutory duties and implement programs that promote a fair and accessible democracy.

Each chapter, as well each profile, seeks to emphasize how critical the state Secretary of State is to ensuring that elections remain free, fair, accessible, and accurate. It is my goal to communicate to all who read these pages just how many current Secretaries are developing innovating agendas to promote those democratic goals. Because one of the other themes that carried through my interviews with several of the Secretaries, and emerges in the following pages, is that in states where Secretaries are elected representatives, voters must hold them directly accountable for protecting the election process. In other words, voters can't forget that they hold the keys to ensuring that their state's chief elections official oversees the election process in a fair, transparent, and judicious manner.

It is my hope that this book will leave voters and engaged citizens better prepared to actively embrace their role as the "employers" of these Secretaries of State.

Chapter 1
The Preeminent Role of the State Secretary of State in Election Administration

> "The thing that gets my heart pounding is standing [up] for every citizens' constitutional right to vote, and working every chance I get to support policies that make it easier for people to vote, and oppose policies that either disenfranchise people or make it more difficult for them to vote. That swells my chest up. If there is a reason to be here, that's it."
>
> Former Oregon Secretary of State Bill Bradbury

Throughout the twentieth century, the role of a state's Secretary of State and their relationship to election administration was relatively unnoticed and publicly unremarkable. At meetings of their national organization, the National Association of Secretaries of State (NASS), the interactions of various State Secretaries of State were described as "friendly" and "free of political bias" and meetings took place out of the public eye, marked with "cooperation, altruism, and deep-seated convictions while acting and reacting to the growing pains of the nation in the 20th Century."[1] One current Secretary, Matt Dunlap of Maine, referred to NASS meetings prior to the 2000 election as a "quiet, friendly little polo club" where Secretaries would "get together and do resolutions in support of each other and it was all good fun." No major controversies, no significant allegations of partisanship, no spotlight.

Then came November 6, 2000. Words like "hanging chad," "punch cards," and "butterfly ballot" inserted themselves into the cultural lexicon, and the only name to rival "Bush" and "Gore" in notoriety was Florida Secretary of State Katherine Harris. Allegations flew over Harris's partiality, pointing in part to the fact that while she was under law charged with overseeing the counting of the ballots and ultimate certification of the vote total between rivals Bush and Gore, she was simultaneously serving as the Florida chairwoman for the Bush–Cheney campaign.

Subsequent chapters address in greater detail the effects of the Katherine Harris spotlight on the evolving roles and expectations for state Secretaries of State. What that spotlight confirmed, however, for the first time in our country's history, was that a state's chief election official plays a significant, if not crucial, role in the administration of democracy.

---

1 *Pillars of Public Service: A History of NASS*, National Association of Secretaries of State, updated 2009, available at: http://nass.org/index.php?option=com_content&task=view&id=40&Itemid=186, at 4, 24.

The Other Players: Congress, State Legislatures, Courts, and Local Administrators

In the seminal case of *Reynolds v. Sims*, 377 U.S. 533 (1964), the United States Supreme Court recognized that "[t]he right to vote freely for the candidate of one's choice is of the essence of a democratic society, and any restrictions on that right strike at the heart of representative government." The Court had noted in a case decided just a few months prior that "No right is more precious in a free country than that of having a voice in the election of those who make the laws under which, as good citizens, we must live. Other rights, even the most basic, are illusory if the right to vote is undermined."[2]

Certainly, multiple entities and actors interact to ensure these principles of democracy are realized throughout the United States. Legislators on the federal and state level draw the parameters of the game, setting minimum requirements for enforcing and protecting citizens' access to free, fair, and accurate elections. But congressional authority to affect elections is fairly limited, state legislatures deliver typically piecemeal solutions that vary greatly from state to state, and legislation emerging out of both entities is more often the product of political maneuvering and reactions to the most recent election controversy. Similarly, federal and state courts have played an increasingly influential role in election administration in recent decades, particularly since the United States Supreme Court decisions in *Baker v. Carr*, 369 U.S. 186 (1962) and *Bush v. Gore*, 531 U.S. 98 (2000). Yet courts are limited to intervening in cases and issues that come before their bench. They are thus inherently reactive, unable to address or proactively improve how elections are administered on a regular basis. And while in many states, local election officials engage in unique and innovative techniques to ensure fair, accessible, and accurate elections, their reach and influence is limited only to their geographical area, and their innovation is in most states cabined by the oversight—direct or indirect—of the state's chief election authority.

So although none of the work of these entities in this context is inconsequential, students of democracy can simply not ignore the significant role that a state Secretary of State, if given the authority over elections, plays in consistently overseeing, interpreting, and implementing election law and democratic principles in their state. Indeed, a state's Secretary of State is not simply charged with running elections, but is responsible for administering them in such a way that effectively promotes interests that are at the heart of a healthy democratic process. Notably, they are primarily responsible for executing policies and programs that further the need to ensure accurate electoral outcomes, including efforts to reduce fraud or intimidation and promote integrity, while also prioritizing access to the vote and enabling the full, uniform, and equal participation of the electorate in the democratic process.

---

2 *Wesberry v. Sanders*, 376 U.S. 1 (1964).

The Congressional Role in Election Administration and Regulation

The role of Congress in election administration is limited by the powers granted to it in the U.S. Constitution. Within those boundaries, policies are executed from afar and, with the exception of some segments of the Voting Rights Act and the National Voter Registration Act, apply uniformly to elections throughout the entire country. As a result, Congress's role is necessarily broad and subject to a significant amount of state and local interpretation.

Under the U.S. Constitution, Congress has explicit authority to make laws regarding the administration of elections for congressional and presidential elections.[3] For instance, Article II grants Congress the power to set the date for presidential elections and some parameters for the Electoral College. Article I, Section 4, the "Elections Clause," grants state legislatures the authority to regulate the "times, places, and manner of holding Elections" for Congress, but grants Congress the ability to "make or alter" these regulations. In Ex Parte Siebold, 100 U.S. 371 (1879), the Supreme Court has interpreted these provisions to apply to presidential elections as well.

It is in furtherance of the power granted under the Elections Clause that Congress enacted the National Voter Registration Act of 1993 (NVRA). The NVRA substantially increased opportunities for voter registration, most significantly through enabling citizens to register to vote in a federal election when they apply for their driver's license, or at various other state offices. But in recognition of state-based variances, the NVRA allowed an exemption for the handful of states that had already enacted same-day voter registration. And though the NVRA directed states to provide and accept completed voter registration forms at certain state agencies, such as any office in the state providing public assistance or state-funded disability, it also allowed for some state discretion in determining which other agencies were to provide registration such as county clerks' offices, public schools, and public libraries. The NVRA also granted states the authority to investigate suspicious voter registration applications and contains detailed regulations for when states may permissibly purge the names of ineligible voters from registration lists. Chapter 3 provides an additional discussion on the specific work that Secretaries of State have taken on to implement or otherwise react to the NVRA.

Congress has a more limited authority in enacting legislation relevant to state and local elections. This role is primarily derived from four separate Constitutional amendments that protect the enfranchisement of individual citizens against specific discriminatory practices in any and all elections based on race, color, previous condition of servitude (the 15th Amendment), gender (the 19th Amendment), age

3 For a general and thorough discussion of the role of Congress in developing and administering election law, see United States General Accounting Office, *The Scope of Congressional Authority in Election Administration* (March 2001). (Online June 2009) available at: http://www.gao.gov/new.items/d01470.pdf (accessed June 9, 2009).

(the 26th Amendment), or the ability to pay a tax. Each of these amendments grants Congress the authority to enforce these prohibitions through appropriate legislation.

Congress's authority to enforce the Fourteenth and Fifteenth Amendments of the U.S. Constitution enabled the passage of the Voting Rights Act in 1965 (VRA), one of the most seminal pieces of legislation in the country's history. The VRA contains several provisions that combine to create a fabric of protection against racial discrimination in all elections, and allows for the appointment of federal observers to monitor compliance. Section 2 protects against discriminatory election laws or practices, prohibiting any voting "qualification … prerequisite … standard, practice, or procedure" that "results in a denial or abridgement of the right of any citizen of the United States to vote on account of race or color." Section 202 prohibits all states and localities from using any "test or device" to establish voter eligibility, including literacy, English proficiency, or character requirements. Section 203 of the VRA requires that certain jurisdictions provide translation assistance for English-learning voters who are of Spanish, Asian, Native American, or Alaska Native descent. Sections 4 and 5 together apply to certain areas of the county—"covered" jurisdictions—that in 1964, 1968, or 1972 required compliance with "any test or device" as a prerequisite to voting. The provisions were designed to prevent the enactment of discriminatory voting procedures by requiring the "pre-clearance" of all new election laws in these covered jurisdictions. To receive pre-clearance, jurisdictions must in part prove to the Attorney General or the U.S. District Court for the District of Columbia that their proposed changes do not have the effect of "retrogressing" or weakening the ability of minority voters in the jurisdiction to participate in the electoral process.

Finally, the Constitution's Spending Clause, spelled out in Article I, empowers Congress to impose certain requirements on states receiving funds from the federal government, so long as those requirements are related to the federal interest that the funding grants are intended to further. Congress was able to enact the Help America Vote Act of 2002 (HAVA) in furtherance of its powers under the Spending Clause. The most significant provisions of HAVA provided funding for states to replace outdated voting machines, required states accepting federal funding to offer provisional ballots and establish state-wide computerized registration lists, and required voters who registered by mail and are participating for the first time to show photo identification, or a copy of a current utility bill, bank statement, government check, paycheck, or other government document that shows their name and address. In addition, HAVA established the Election Assistance Commission and established uniform requirements for all voting systems used in federal elections. These latter requirements mandate that all voting systems purchased with the federal funds permit the voter an opportunity to verify and change or correct their vote, alert voters of when they've over-voted, and produce a permanent paper record with manual audit capacity that could serve as the official record in the event of a recount.

The Role of Federal Courts in Election Administration and Regulation

In recent years the impression that federal courts may seem to be playing an increasingly large role in overseeing the electoral process has gained increased attention, due in no small part to the U.S. Supreme Court's majority opinion in *Bush v. Gore*. But the role that federal courts play in regulating elections was a source of debate and controversy long before the 2000 presidential election. The evolution of voting as a fundamental right under the U.S. Constitution originated in the 1962 Supreme Court case of *Baker v. Carr*, in which the Court established that equal protection challenges to redistricting plans were justiciable under the Fourteenth Amendment. The Court's subsequent analysis two years later in *Reynolds v. Sims* specifically articulated the use of a strict scrutiny analysis in evaluating any laws that potentially infringe on "the right to exercise the franchise in a free and unimpaired manner." Under this strict scrutiny standard, a state is required to demonstrate a compelling interest and show that its law affecting a fundamental right is narrowly tailored to serve that interest. The *Reynolds* analysis carried a significant presumption against any state election law that abridges a fundamental right, and it is rare for a law to survive such scrutiny.

Roughly twenty years after *Reynolds*, the Supreme Court introduced the concept of a more flexible scrutiny of some state election laws and procedures in *Anderson v. Celebrezze*, 460 U.S. 780 (1983). The Court in *Anderson* was asked to determine whether an early filing deadline for presidential candidates in Ohio that arguably made it difficult for independent candidates to appear on the ballot placed an unconstitutional burden on the voting and associational rights of independent candidates and their supporters. In upholding the filing deadline, the Court pointed to the clause in Article I of the U.S. Constitution that grants states the power to establish the time, place, and manner of holding federal elections for Senators and Representatives. The court concluded that any challenge to a state election law must evaluate "the character and magnitude of the asserted injury to the rights protected by the First and Fourteenth Amendments" against "the precise interests put forward by the State as justifications for the burden imposed by its rule." To this end, the *Anderson* court stated that the state's vague but "important" interest in regulating elections is "generally sufficient to justify reasonable, nondiscriminatory restrictions."

This increased recognition of the state's interest in promoting a particular election law or procedure was underscored in the U.S. Supreme Court's 1992 decision in *Burdick v. Takushi*, 504 U.S. 428 (1992). In *Burdick*, the Court applied the more relaxed scrutiny articulated in *Anderson* and upheld a state law that prohibited write-in voting. The Court concluded that Hawaii's prohibition on write-in voting did not unreasonably infringe upon its citizens' rights under the First and Fourteenth Amendments. The Supreme Court reasoned that all election laws "invariably impose some burden upon individual voters" and that subjecting "every voting regulation to strict scrutiny and [requiring] that the regulation be narrowly tailored to advance a compelling state interest [ties] the hands of States seeking to assure that elections are operated equitably and efficiently." The court emphasized *Anderson*'s "more flexible standard," reasoning that a state's regulatory interests are "generally sufficient to justify" any reasonable, nondiscriminatory restrictions upon the fundamental right to vote.

In 2008, the court continued down this line of reasoning in its review of Indiana's photo identification requirement for voters in *Crawford v. Marion County Election Board*, 128 S. Ct. 1610 (2008). In *Crawford* the Court upheld the requirement as facially constitutional, reiterating its position that "evenhanded restrictions" geared towards protecting the "integrity and reliability of the electoral process" are acceptable under the Constitution.[4]

The *Crawford* Court also looked to *Burdick* and reasoned that "when we consider only the [Indiana] statute's broad application to all Indiana voters we conclude that it 'imposes only a limited burden on voters' rights.'"[5] The Court went on to conclude that "[t]he 'precise interests' advanced by [Indiana] are therefore sufficient to defeat petitioners' facial challenge to [the statute]."[6] Indiana's asserted state interests of participating in a "nationwide effort to improve and modernize election procedures," deterrence and detection of voter fraud, and protecting public confidence in elections were "unquestionably relevant to its interest in protecting the integrity and reliability of the electoral process."[7] The Court also weighed the burdens imposed on eligible voters who lacked the photo ID card necessary to comply with the statute, and determined that because a photo identification card was available free of charge that the burdens imposed in obtaining one "[do] not qualify as a substantial burden on the right to vote, or even represent a significant increase over the usual burdens of voting."[8]

Thus while *Anderson*, *Burdick*, and *Crawford* represented a modern tendency for federal courts to grant greater deference to state laws that regulate elections, *Bush v. Gore* marked, among other things, a reinvigoration of the court's oversight of the electoral process under the Equal Protection Clause. The opinion overturned a decision by the Florida Supreme Court that ordered, among other things, a statewide manual recount of all registered undervotes cast for the presidency in Florida during the 2000 presidential election. Though only five Justices agreed that the recount should not go forward based on their interpretation of the Electoral Count Act,[9] seven joined a per curiam opinion that held the Equal Protection Clause

---

4 *Crawford v. Marion County Election Board Bd.*, 128 S. Ct. 1610, 1616 (2008) (quoting *Anderson v. Celebrezze*, 460 U.S. 780, 788, n. 9 (1983)).

5 *Crawford*, 128 S. Ct. at 1623 (quoting *Burdick*, 504 U.S. at 439).

6 *Id.* at 1623 (quoting *Burdick*, 504 U.S. at 434).

7 *Id.* at 1616–17.

8 *Id.* at 1621.

9 United States General Accounting Office, March 2001, *supra* note 3, at 110. For an extensive analysis of the details surrounding this aspect of the *Bush v. Gore* holding, see Richard L. Pildes, *The Law of Presidential Elections: Issues in the Wake of Florida 2000: Judging "New Law" in Election Disputes*, 29 Fla. St. U.L. Rev. 691 (2001); Lawrence H.

of the Fourteenth Amendment required the creation and enforcement of uniform standards to guide individuals in counting ballots and votes during the statewide manual recount. This per curiam opinion reasoned that the Equal Protection Clause protects not only "the initial allocation of the franchise" but "applies as well to the manner of its exercise." The court concluded that when a state enacts policies that arbitrarily and disparately "value one person's vote over that of another," it violates the Fourteenth Amendment.

This new view of the Equal Protection Clause as it relates to voting is being applied in a handful of subsequent federal court opinions. In *Stewart v. Blackwell*, 444 F.3d 843 (6th Cir. 2006), superseded en banc by 473 F.3d 692 (6th Cir. 2007), a three-judge panel on the Sixth Circuit Court of Appeals required a strict scrutiny of Ohio's decision to allow the use of different ballot machines in counties throughout the state. Because some of these counties used punch card machines, which were shown to the court to have a higher error rate in counting ballots, and because the state could show no compelling interest to justify its allowance of the use of these punch card machines, the panel reasoned that the disparate use and allocations of the machines violated the *Bush v. Gore* view of the Equal Protection Clause. The decision was later vacated as moot by the full court.[10] But the following year, the Sixth Circuit invoked this rationale again in *League of Women Voters v. Brunner*, 548 F.3d 463 (6th Cir. 2008). In that opinion, a three judge panel re-emphasized the central tenet of *Bush v. Gore* that prohibits a state's ability to, "by later arbitrary and disparate treatment, value one person's vote over that of another." In the *Brunner* case, the Sixth Circuit specifically held that varieties in election administration throughout Ohio, such as forcing people in some parts of the state to wait many hours to vote as a consequence of the arbitrary allocation of voting machines, for instance, would violate Equal Protection.

Amongst this ever-evolving jurisprudence regulating the parameters of their intervention in election administration, federal courts, like Congress, maintain a primary role as overseer in ensuring that state and federal authorities regulate elections in compliance with the Court's view of constitutional duties and limitations. And like Congress, this role is not only limited by the U.S. Constitution and any relevant statutes, it is primarily reactive and deferential to the actions of officials on the state and local level. Indeed, the Supreme Court articulated the effect of this deference, being that states "have evolved comprehensive, and in many respects complex, election codes regulating in

---

Tribe, *eroG v. hsuB and Its Disguises: Freeing Bush v. Gore from Its Hall of Mirrors*, 115 Harvard. L. Rev. 170 (2001).

10 Similarly, in *Southwest Voter Registration Education Project v. Shelley*, 344 F.3d 882, 894–95 (9th Cir. 2003), vacated en banc, 344 F.3d 914 (9th Cir. 2003), a three judge panel on the Ninth Circuit Court of Appeals applied strict scrutiny to conclude that the sporadic use of punch card machines violated the Equal Protection Clause. But the Ninth Circuit voted to review the three judge panel decision in *Shelley* en banc, and subsequently reversed the decision.

most substantial ways, with respect to both federal and state elections, the time, place, and manner of holding primary and general elections, the registration and qualifications of voters, and the selection and qualification of candidates."[11]

The Role of State Legislatures in Election Administration and Regulation

While the federal role in elections is cabined by the parameters of federalism, state legislatures are the primary source of laws regulating the electoral process. State legislatures are responsible for enacting laws, where constitutionally permissible, on everything from ballot access and registration requirements, voter identification requirements, the date and time of state elections, the casting of absentee ballots, campaign finance regulations, and methods of counting, recounting, and auditing election results. State legislatures also can establish remedies and punishments for violations of these laws, and can empower state authorities and agencies, such as the State Attorney General or the Secretary of State, to monitor or investigate violations of the election code.

State legislatures grant—either explicitly through legislation, or implicitly through silence—a varying range of discretion to the state and local officials that are charged with administering and supervising elections. In addition, the legislative development of state election codes also varies widely from state to state. Some states, for example, do not allow individuals convicted of certain crimes to vote, even after their sentences are completed, while many others only restrict offenders who are currently incarcerated. Eight states—Maine, Montana, Minnesota, Wisconsin, Wyoming, Idaho, New Hampshire, and Iowa—allow voters to register to vote on Election Day. Many neighboring states require citizens to register to vote thirty days before their first election. A handful of states require voters to present photo identification before they receive a ballot on Election Day, while most others only require identification for first time voters under federal law.

The state-to-state variance in election laws illuminates another aspect to the process which is that the state's passage of laws can be piecemeal, sporadic, and dominated or driven by partisan concerns. Such a system, void of consistency and sometimes even logic, has led at least one commentator to lament that this vast "diversity of systems" reflects either "a thriving example of federalist experimentation or a horrifying mishmash of self-serving behavior."[12]

The Role of State Courts in Election Administration and Regulation

In his speech entitled "The Role of State Courts in the Battle for Inclusive Participation in the Electoral Process," Judge George Bundy Smith, a sitting judge

11 *Storer v. Brown*, 415 U.S. 724, 730 (U.S. 1974).

12 *Note: Toward a Greater State Role in Election Administration*, 118 Harv. L. Rev. 2314, 2315 (2005).

on the New York Court of Appeals, argued that the primary role of both state judges is twofold. Like federal judges, they are "required to maintain constant vigilance to ensure that the level playing field promised by Justice Brennan in *Baker v. Carr* becomes and remains a reality." This primarily entails, in his view, ensuring that the one person one vote principle is preserved and enforced. In addition, state judges must ensure "that the Federal Constitution, state constitutions, and the Voting Rights Act are enforced to prevent discrimination against African Americans and other minorities." In furthering this responsibility, Judge Smith reasons, the court must ensure that "the playing field is the same for all of those who play a part in determining the electoral winner."

To that end, state courts occupy a precarious position in the world of election law. On one hand, they are charged under every state constitution with resolving disputes or punishing violations of the election code that the state legislature develops and the state election official administers, but it is rare for a state court to intervene to overturn an electoral outcome. State elections codes usually empower their courts to invalidate elections when it is impossible to determine the legal outcome,[13] or when an election is irreparably tainted with fraud. But state court intervention more typically amounts to ordering a recount, disqualifying or decertifying absentee ballots, issuing a declaration regarding the counting of certain ballots as "legal" votes, or issuing criminal sanctions against individuals, including campaign officials and election officials, who commit an act such as voter fraud, manipulation, or intimidation.[14]

Yet on the other hand, state courts are often the most effective and influential in addressing the type of enforcement that Judge Smith identifies in his speech. But, like federal courts, they are reactive and thus less effective in influencing election administration on a regular basis. As a Note in the Harvard Law Review observed, though court intervention may cast a "shadow" over the duties of election officials, courts generally set "wide boundaries within which local officials have broad discretion." The Note contends that, for example, it is rare for state courts to "unseat a victor declared by a state election process." As a result, any subsequent "hue and cry in the courts is largely futile: state and local bureaucrats single-handedly translate voter action into virtually final electoral outcomes."

The Role of Local Election Officials

Finally, local election officials and administrators—clerks, election judges, local election boards, and the like—undoubtedly play a role in the grassroots implementation of election law and policy. Importantly, this responsibility,

13 See *Akizaki v. Fong*, 51 Haw. 354 (1969).

14 For a more extensive analysis of various cases where state courts intervene to enforce state election laws, see Samuel Issacharrof, Pamela S. Karlan and Richard H. Pildes, *The Law of Democracy* chs 12–13 (3rd edn, 2007).

discretion, and power of the Secretary of State can even dwarf that of local election officials. Many states place a significant amount of responsibility for the nuts and bolts of election administration in the hands of local government officials. These officials often are responsible for the actual recruitment, hiring, and training of individuals who are working at the polls on Election Day, often process voter registration forms, and provide voters with information about voting procedures.

Yet in nearly every state, the statewide officials are empowered with some extent of control over the local authorities. In Vermont, for example, elections are run "town by town" by the town clerks. But as Vermont Secretary of State Deborah Markowitz noted, these town clerks have many other duties and rely on her office "entirely" for direction and support: "we train them, we provide step-by-step training manuals, we provide all of the supplies they need, and through rule making and working with the legislature we also establish what the rules are in running an election." And though it is rare, her office has the authority to intervene on Election Day to correct any local mishaps.

In most states, it is the state level authority that certifies all statewide election results and in some states, such as Rhode Island, Secretaries of State have the power to remove local election officials. Some statewide officials are responsible for supporting local officials with financial resources, many administer certification courses for local administrators or assist in some way with poll worker recruitment and training. The bottom line is that local election administrators are closest to the ground when it comes to running elections, and they certainly play a unique and important role in running elections. But in nearly every state they work either under the direction or influence of the statewide administrators who oversee them and the process.

The Role of the State Secretary of State in Election Administration and Regulation

When Bill Gardner was first elected to the New Hampshire state legislature in 1972, election reform was on the minds of many in the legislature. As a state legislator, Gardner put forward a series of proposals to improve election administration in New Hampshire, following a particularly controversial election. Merits aside, not one of then-state legislator Gardner's election reform proposals was successfully enacted into law. A few years later, in the summer of 1976, there was an opening in the New Hampshire Secretary of State office, a position that in New Hampshire is filled by a majority vote of the state legislature. Gardner ran for the position and was elected. In his first term as Secretary of State, Gardner re-submitted all of his election reform proposals that the state legislature had rejected a few years earlier. Now championed by a sitting Secretary, nearly every proposal passed.

Gardner's experience illuminates the unique leadership authority that a state's chief election official or entity, typically the Secretary of State, can play in the democratic process. Each state has either an individual or an appointed board that works at the statewide level with all of the above entities to ensure that elections are administered in a way that furthers the principles of democracy. They work at once to support and comply with federal constitutional and statutory requirements, implement state constitutional and legislative mandates and principles, and oversee and support the work of local officials. In each of the above discussions—the roles of Congress, federal courts, state legislatures, and state courts—the Secretary of State bears a great deal of the burden of ensuring nearly each piece of legislation or almost every court order they establish meets its practical goals. They are the ultimate election coordinators, working with all relevant entities to ensure the smooth and efficient administration of elections throughout the state.

And while there are differences and the range of their authority in practice from state to state, in nearly every one of the thirty-six states where the Secretary of State oversees the implementation of elections, it is clear that they are able to exert significant leadership and authority and influence over implementing the intent, goals, and policies of every other governmental entity involved in the electoral process. They serve as generals in administering or effectuating the goals of Congress, state legislatures, and the courts. But because they often possess a great deal of independent discretion to interpret or proactively fill in the gaps of the parameters laid out by these other entities, the most effective Secretaries adhere not only to compliance and coordination with other authorities. They also take steps to proactively effectuate the larger goals of a healthy democracy—including promoting access to participation, accurate outcomes, and the accountability of elected officials throughout the state.

For example, particularly since the enactment of the Help America Vote Act in 2002, Secretaries of State are able to wield influence over the implementation of voter identification requirements, the methods and ease of voter registration, and the maintenance of voter registration lists, along with any relevant voter education around these and other issues. And again, to be sure, state and federal courts, legislatures, and Congress have some authority over advancing, evaluating, or enforcing policies in each of these areas. But the Secretary of State occupies a crucial position in implementing these policies. As such, they play a pivotal role in ensuring that each policy is administered and applied to ensure accuracy, access, and accountability in the political process.

And on Election Day local election officials and poll workers take center stage, but a Secretary of State is uniquely positioned to work with local officials to ensure that all state and federal laws are followed and that voters' experiences are consistent throughout the state. In addition, the Secretary may also have the power to set goals, such as limits on ballot spoilage rates and wait times, decorum at precinct polling locations, assistance for English-learning voters, or other guidelines for local officials to follow that promote accuracy, uniformity, and access. In many states, for example, Secretaries of State are the primary decision maker in selecting voting machines, ensuring they are impervious to misuse, and providing training for all local officials and, potentially, all poll workers. Specific examples of Secretaries proactively implementing and administering those types of Election Day policies are provided throughout the course of this book. Finally, because some of the problems that occur on Election Day may be unpredictable, this section also considers the importance and rapidity of the Secretary of State's response to any snafus that occur throughout the day. From precincts running out of ballots to challengers causing a ruckus at the polls, a statewide election official who is aware of and quickly responds to address—or help address—any mishaps can play a pivotal role in presenting any Election Day meltdowns.

Leadership and Qualifications of Recent State Secretaries of State

Given the significant responsibility of a Secretary of State in implementing democracy, it is crucial that the individuals who fill these roles are equipped with a full understanding of their responsibilities *vis-à-vis* the electoral process. For unlike the entities described above, the Secretary occupies a unique position in the administration of democracy. Because they have a significant amount of discretion in administering state and federal mandates, coupled with their authority or influence over the actions of local officials, not only must they be familiar with their legal responsibilities, they also have the opportunity, if not the obligation, to be proactive, creative, and innovative leaders in promoting and ensuring accessible, accurate, and accountable elections.

So who are these critical guardians of democracy? With the exception of New Hampshire Secretary Bill Gardner, in office continually since the legislature first elected him in 1976, all were elected after 1990. Notably, twenty-nine were elected or appointed in the years following the 2000 presidential election and the illumination of Florida Secretary of State Katherine Harris as a central player in the Florida recount. Before the 2000 election, in the words of Vermont Secretary of State Deborah Markowitz (elected in 1998), only her office and local election officials "cared or were interested in the nuts and bolts of how we run our democracy." Since then, an increasing number of Secretaries have been elected based upon their experience in or intention to advance reforms to the democratic system.

A survey of the thirty-six Secretaries serving in 2009 who oversee elections in their respective states indicates, just as in other office holders, they have varied backgrounds and qualifications, with some similarities. Seven are former local election administrators, and at least eight served time in their respective states' legislatures or in other state or local political offices prior to their ascendancy to the Secretary of State position. And almost half came to their job with law degrees and many were practicing attorneys prior to their election or appointment.

When asked what aspect of their background was most informative of their work administering elections, those with law degrees unanimously cited their understanding of the law and the election code as critical. Louisiana Secretary of State Jay Dardenne credits his background as an attorney and his time in the state legislature overseeing the office of Secretary of State as being the "most beneficial" to helping prepare him for his position. Nevada Secretary of State Ross Miller described his law degree as "invaluable, just for the simple fact that so much of what we do is ask to interpret statutes, ask to try to clarify what the statutes are, what the policy is going to be moving forward, [and] to issue interpretations." Miller also noted that "a good portion" of his work with regards to elections involves responding to "complaints from major law firms or trying to respond to requests for interpretations of the statutes," work for which his legal background has been uniquely useful. Oregon Secretary of State Bill Bradbury echoed that sentiment, noting that the law is "the fundamental underpinning" to election administration and that because "there are lots of ways to interpret the law, it becomes very critical that I implement the law [and] work very hard to make sure that people are enabled to vote." California Secretary of State Debra Bowen similarly noted that for Secretaries "working to stay scrupulously nonpartisan" knowing the law enables them to "simply take the law and carry out [their] duties under the law." Bowen's understanding of the California election code has led her to, among other things, notice that it needs updating, and she's made it part of her work in office to "clean up" the law.

And Nebraska Secretary of State John Gale simply stated: "I don't think I would enjoy this nearly as much as I do if I wasn't an attorney." Gale noted that when he was running for the position, a previous Secretary of State who was not an attorney told him that "it really will help you immensely as a secretary of state if you are an attorney," in part because he would "enjoy the legal things." Gale said that being a lawyer enabled him to "understand fully the whole concept of due process of law and what we have to do to have a fair hearing. If I wasn't an attorney some of those areas maybe much more blurred and I would be more at risk of making mistakes and making bad judgments." For instance, he explained that of his many duties as Secretary, "require an active understanding of the law, and an active understanding of due process of law: [including] How to conduct a fair hearing, [and] how you ensure that everyone is treated fairly." Gale views his position as Secretary as a "quasi-judge, because various questions come to me that I have to resolve as a legal matter." And as an attorney, he is able to make those decisions or issue interpretations of the law in a neutral way by focusing on constitutional issues and, as a judge would, "quarantining" himself from lobbyists or special interest groups, rejecting phone calls and visitors who want to address the issue, and isolating himself from any partisan pressures to make a "pure legal decision."

While Vermont Secretary of State Deborah Markowitz called her background as an attorney "a tremendous asset," both she and former West Virginia Secretary of State Betty Ireland emphasized the usefulness of their previous work as an educator as similarly helpful. Iowa Secretary of State Michael Mauro and Washington Secretary of State Sam Reed cited their background as election administrators and overall passion for the work of overseeing elections as their most important qualification. Both experiences enable a Secretary to fulfill an important role, which Markowitz articulated as the ability for local election administrators "to call someone who knows more than they do" about election law and administration. For in her view and others, a crucial role of the Secretary is to provide leadership to local election administrators in the state, other government officials, and voters themselves. As Wyoming Secretary Max Maxfield and Kansas Secretary Ron Thornburgh both noted, there are no "do-overs". In Maxfield's view, "if somebody calls this office with a specific question relating to an election item, we've got to get it right the first time." And in Thornburgh's view, Secretaries "spend a lot of time talking about access and security, and I think as we try to balance what we're doing right now, this really is rocket science in that you have to get it right the first time."

Markowitz expanded on her view of that leadership, describing it in two ways:

> "one is that we have the power of the soap box, the ability to talk about issues, the importance of voting and participation, the ability to get schools to actually teach civics education, to get businesses to release workers to go to vote, to get unions to make [the registration of all their members] part of their platform, those kinds of things. Just by using the [bully] pulpit to talk about these values and these goals, I think you can make a significant impact on participation in the state. That's one place of leadership. The other place of leadership is taking a proactive approach. And so, what we have done in every election cycle, or every few years we'll look at census data and we'll look at national studies that tell us who isn't voting. And then we work with other organizations that are interested in voter turnout to look at ways that we can begin to reach those non-voting populations."

Similarly, Iowa Secretary Michael Mauro discussed the importance of being able to talk to voters about the election process, answering questions from audiences confused by media reports about stolen elections. When he travels around Iowa to talk about the election process, he sees the audience "perk up" and pepper him with questions about whether their vote will count or "how do I know it's going to be counted, what happened in Ohio, what happened in Florida, how do you explain these things, why isn't there a paper trail, tell us about the touch screen machines." Mauro uses his bully pulpit to educate and empower voters with an understanding of how the administration process works.

And Secretary Reed echoed Markowitz's point about taking a proactive approach, detailing the importance of inspiring local election administrators "to go beyond the statutory requirements to do more voter outreach, connecting with the people, and voter information, and getting more registration participation." Nebraska Secretary John Gale described his work as being "very aggressive and proactive about voter education and voter outreach," often creating "new programs that try to reach different elements of our society [and] to be in effect a cheerleader [for] good citizenship." Gale does a media tour of the state before every major election to talk about the election process and the importance and value of voting. His tour seeks to "engage with people and help them to realize that freedom isn't free and democracy really does require the participation of every citizen at every level."

Other Secretaries described their own leadership in various ways. Alabama Secretary of State Beth Chapman refers to her role as the "air traffic controller," Indiana Secretary Todd Rokita described it as leading an army, and West Virginia Secretary Betty Ireland referred to herself as the "visible face of elections" in her state. South Dakota Secretary of State Chris Nelson emphasized that "the number one thing that the Secretary of State can do is set the tone [within their state] for how elections are going to be conducted, and set the expectation for the county election officials that it will be done right, it will be fair, [and that] we will do everything it takes in order to accomplish those two goals."

In addition to these individual anecdotes, what emerges from several discussions with Secretaries about their roles is the unique ability of a Secretary of State to provide needed leadership on issues of election administration. Whether they were previously a state legislator, educator, election administrator, attorney, business leader, fur trapper,[15] those that bring a passion to the position and embrace its leadership opportunities appear to be the most effective at using the office to achieve greater engagement and confidence of voters throughout the state.

15 Of all the varying backgrounds and qualifications of current or recent Secretaries of State, none matches that of Matt Dunlap, whose prior positions, according to his official biography, included "extensive work as a cook, a bartender and bar manager, radio show host, proofreader, research assistant, waiter, editor, writer, fur trapper, and textile worker."

Background and Party Affiliation of Secretaries of State Serving in 2009

State	Secretary	Year Elected	Party Affiliation	Background
Alabama	Beth Chapman	2006	Republican	State Auditor
Arizona	Jan Brewer	2002	Republican	Legislator
Arkansas	Charlie Daniels	2002	Democrat	Land Commissioner
California	Debra Bowen	2006	Democrat	Law, Legislator
Colorado	Bernie Buescher	2009	Democrat	Legislator
Connecticut	Susan Bysiewicz	1998	Democrat	Law, Legislator
Florida	Kurt Browning	2006	Republican	Elections
Georgia	Karen Handel	2006	Republican	Business, Politics
Idaho	Ben Ysursa	2002	Republican	Law, Elections
Indiana	Todd Rokita	2002	Republican	Law
Iowa	Michael Mauro	2006	Democrat	Elections, Education
Kansas	Ron Thornburgh	1994	Republican	Elections
Kentucky	Trey Grayson	2002	Republican	Law
Louisiana	Jay Dardenne	2006	Republican	Law, Legislator
Maine	Matt Dunlap	2004	Democrat	Legislator
Massachusetts	Bill Galvin	1994	Democrat	Law
Michigan	Terri Lynn Land	2002	Republican	Elections
Minnesota	Mark Ritchie	2006	Democrat	Civic Nonprofit
Mississippi	Delbert Hosemann	2007	Republican	Law
Missouri	Robin Carnahan	2004	Democrat	Law
Montana	Linda McCulloch	2008	Democrat	Education
Nebraska	John Gale	2002	Republican	Law
Nevada	Ross Miller	2006	Democrat	Law
New Hampshire	Bill Gardner	1976	Democrat	Legislator
New Mexico	Mary Herrera	2006	Democrat	Elections
North Dakota	Al Jaeger	1992	Republican	Real Estate
Ohio	Jennifer Brunner	2006	Democrat	Law
Oregon	Kate Brown	2008	Democrat	Law, Legislator
Pennsylvania	Pedro Cortés	2003	Democrat	Law
Rhode Island	Ralph Mollis	2006	Democrat	Law, Mayor
South Dakota	Chris Nelson	2002	Republican	Elections
Texas	Hope Andrade	2008	Republican	Business
Vermont	Deborah Markowitz	1998	Democrat	Law
Washington	Sam Reed	2000	Republican	Elections
West Virginia	Natalie Tennant	2008	Democrat	Media
Wyoming	Max Maxfield	2006	Republican	State Auditor

New Hampshire Secretary of State Bill Gardner

First Elected: 1976

If you want to know what controversies will plague election administration in the future, just ask New Hampshire Secretary of State Bill Gardner. Since taking office in 1976, Gardner has anticipated and acted to protect voters in his state against election problems—years, sometimes decades, before the rest of the country catches wind of the problem.

Case in point: punch card ballots. After overseeing several recounts in close elections in his state in the 1980s, where hanging chads and dimpled ballots rendered the results as accurate as a coin toss, Gardner led an effort to successfully ban punch card voting in his state. It would be another twenty years, in the 2000 election, before the rest of the country learned what Gardner already knew: punch cards caused problems.

New Hampshire is one of three states where the legislature elects one of their own to serve as the State Secretary of State. When Gardner sought the position in the summer of 1976, he met with several of the most respected legislators serving at the time to tell them that he was considering running for the position. In his words: "I picked a half a dozen that I respected and I went to them and I said that I was considering running for this position. And I told them what I thought my liabilities were, I was young, and most of the legislators were older, and I was a Democrat and most of the legislators were Republicans, but that I cared about the elections process. I asked them what they thought. Everyone told me basically the same thing. Not one of them said they would vote for me. I was not considered really a serious candidate. It was sort of a joke. But I won."

Gardner has since become one of the longest serving and most highly revered state Secretaries of State in the history of the United States. He is often mentioned as a mentor to many current and recent Secretaries, like Ross Miller of Nevada. When asked to discuss Gardner, Miller reverently remarked that when asked, Gardner is able to recall the historical background of nearly every election reform or controversy in the country's history. To Miller, and others, Gardner "is the elder statesman of the Secretaries of State."

Chapter 2
The Secretary and the Political Party

"I think that we are, as a group, and I say this for Republicans and Democrats, we all take our jobs extremely seriously. And those of us who handle elections, we understand that we've got to be mindful of going the extra mile to not just be fair and judicious, but to actually make sure that people know that we are."

Georgia Secretary of State Karen Handel

On May 20, 2008, NBC News Chief Foreign Affairs Correspondent Andrea Mitchell issued an observation that stunned the election administration community. Commenting on problems in previous elections, Mitchell hinted that in the November 2008 general election, Republican Secretaries of State in historically "red states" might seek to prevent a fair vote. In Mitchell's view then-Senator Barack Obama "has to figure out a way to get a fair vote if he's the nominee in those red states" because of the potential for "Katherine Harris-type election officials" in those states to tamper with the election results.[1]

Several Secretaries were aghast after hearing of Mitchell's statement. Speaking for many of them, the National Association of Secretaries of State (NASS) issued a scathing rebuke,[2] calling Mitchell's remarks "speculative" and "unacceptable and unfair to all election officials whose integrity was seemingly called into question solely upon the basis of their political party affiliation." NASS pointed to a resolution passed by a majority of its Secretaries of State in 2005 to decline to serve on political campaign committees or publicly endorse candidates for office. The statement also noted that because "our members—regardless of political party affiliation—strive to deliver fair, accurate and impartial elections during the 2008 presidential election cycle and beyond, we respectfully demand that journalists be held to the same high standards of integrity and objectivity."

Recalling his own reaction, Wyoming Secretary Max Maxfield, a Republican, chided that he's "been a political junkie since [getting] kicked out of the fifth grade for carrying a banner into a voting place." But calmly and seriously, Maxfield described Mitchell's statement as "painfully" inaccurate. In his state, he noted, "even if I wanted to set out today to influence any county, on any election, I could not swing one vote."

---

1 National Association of Secretaries of State (NASS) Statement on Remarks Made by NBC News Correspondent Andrea Mitchell: Secretaries of State Disappointed by Journalist's Suggestion that Election Officials Will Prevent a Fair Election.

2 *Id.*

Yet Mitchell's remark—fair or not—epitomized a cloud of suspicion that hangs over election administration in the United States. The controversy surrounding the 2000 election shattered many voters' faith in the elections process. And in the post-2000 world of elections, it is impossible to embark on any discussion of the role of a state Secretary of State in administering democracy without addressing questions of how they handle or avoid the appearance of partisanship and partiality.

It's been called the "Katherine Harris effect,"[3] the suspicion that many Secretaries of State are nefariously working behind the scenes to tinker with the electoral process and ensure that their political party wins elections in their state. The "effect" originated in November 2000. On the 26th day of that month, nearly three weeks since the historic and confusing Election Day, Florida Secretary of State Katherine Harris certified the results of her state's election contest and declared, in a live press conference, that Texas Governor George W. Bush had won Florida's 25 electoral votes, thus ensuring he would win the Presidency. And her declaration was delivered amidst allegations that she was, in a word, biased. Among other things, critics pointed to the fact that tens of thousands of voters had been wrongfully removed from Florida's registration lists on her watch, along with her decisions to reject recount protests and late-filed election returns.

These and other allegations provided the backdrop for a deeper suspicion. Was the Republican Harris really working all along to use her position as the state's chief election official to help Republican Bush win Florida's coveted electoral college votes? After all, she was more than just the co-chair of George W. Bush's Florida election campaign. She served as a delegate to the 2000 Republican National Convention. She campaigned for Bush during the New Hampshire primary.[4] She stored Republican Party campaign documents, including talking points supporting Bush, on her state-owned office computers. And investigations into her phone records later revealed that she had been in contact with George W. Bush's campaign and his brother, Republican Governor Jeb Bush, throughout the Florida dispute.[5]

Speculations about Harris aside, many came to suspect that political parties were recognizing the power of a Secretary of State to use their office and role as chief elections official to swing votes for their party. Maine Secretary of State Matt Dunlap, who was serving in the Maine state legislature at the time, recalled that "word on the street" following the 2000 election was a "sense that the Republicans suddenly saw the Secretary of State not as a sleepy position, but a critical player on the team. This is the set up man now, not just another relief pitcher. And there was a strong effort to increase the team players." Indeed, in 2002, the first

3 Ann Shorstein, *Politicizing the Election Process: The Katherine Harris Effect*, 2 Fl. Coastal L.J. 373 (2001).

4 For more information on the allegations of partisanship that surrounded Katherine Harris during the 2000 Presidential Election, see *id.*

5 Richard L. Hasen, *Beyond the Margin of Litigation: Reforming U.S. Election Administration to Avoid Electoral Meltdown*, 62 Wash. & Lee L. Rev. 937, 958 (2005).

election following the 2000 presidential election, voters in eight states elected new Secretaries of State. Republicans won in seven of the states.

Whether the "word on the street" was more than rumor and conjecture, four years later, history nearly repeated itself in Ohio. Similar to Florida's role in deciding the 2000 presidential election, in 2004 Ohio was the ultimate swing state. Many believed that as went Ohio, so went the election. And running Ohio's elections at the time? Republican Secretary of State Kenneth Blackwell.

Like Harris, Blackwell served as Ohio's chief elections official while chairing the Ohio campaign for President Bush's re-election bid and actively campaigned in support of a ballot initiative to ban gay marriage. In the weeks leading up to Election Day 2004, Blackwell issued several decisions that provoked multiple lawsuits, including disputes over his enforcement of a statute allowing Republican challengers inside precincts on Election Day, and decisions to alter requirements for accepting voter registration cards. When President George W. Bush won re-election with Ohio's electoral votes, many pundits and commentators pointed to Blackwell's policies as helping Bush win Ohio, and the presidential election.[6]

But in 2006, the tide began to shift. Katherine Harris lost her bid to become a U.S. Senator, Blackwell failed in his effort to be elected Ohio Governor, and Minnesota Secretary of State Mary Kiffmeyer, referred to by one Secretary as "the mother hen of the cabal of very partisan Republican Secretaries," lost her bid for re-election to Democrat Mark Ritchie. Ritchie, who had never before held elected office, but worked as the former director of a nonpartisan civic engagement nonprofit, ran on a reform agenda of fairness and impartiality.

At the same time, in contrast to 2002, seven of the eleven new Secretaries of State elected in 2006 were Democrats—a trend that was repeated in 2008, when all three newly elected Secretaries were Democrats. An August 2006 article in USA Today, for example, highlighted efforts by "national Democratic groups … unhappy about Harris' decisions and those of Republican Kenneth Blackwell in Ohio two years ago" to "pour resources" into several Secretary of State races.[7] The Democrats, it would seem, had taken a page from the Republican playbook and were now similarly focusing on the recruitment and support of left-leaning Secretaries. But, as Maine Secretary Matt Dunlap, a Democrat, observed, "for a partisan Democrat elected under those auspices, what is their freedom to act independently if they owe some of their election to the partisan acts of others?"

In 2008, Dunlap reasoned that "[m]any of the Republicans I was wary of four years ago because of their partisan leanings I have since found to do a pretty good job." While what Dunlap calls the "spy versus spy game" between parties may have

6 See, e.g., Pete Shuler, *Ken Blackwell's Disgraceful Election Machinations*, Dec. 8, 2004, CityBeat, http://www.citybeat.com/cincinnati/article-9128-ken-blackwells-disgraceful-election-machinations.html (declaring that "Every significant decision that Ohio Secretary of State Ken Blackwell made regarding the 2004 presidential election benefited George W. Bush").

7 Jill Lawrence, *Top Vote Counter Becomes Prize Job*, USA Today, Aug. 17, 2006.

leveled out, the years since the 2000 election have, according to Dunlap, "only hurt our ability to convey a sense of integrity in what we're doing to the public." But given Andrea Mitchell's comment, and the public perception it invites or alludes to, the question remains: what can be done moving forward to ensure that a state's chief elections official is insulated from partisan politics? Is the solution to make the position an appointed one, as Florida chose to do after the Harris brouhaha? Or is it, as several academics, legal commentators, politicians, and others have recommended,[8] better to ensure that the position is nonpartisan, and thus insulated from any loyalties to a political party that supported their election?

Secretaries of State and Perceptions of Partisanship

Prior to examining potential reforms to addressing partisan influences on the ability of Secretaries to win elections, it is worth examining the allegations and effects of partisan bias—perceived or actual—on the democratic process. Actual bias could manifest itself in one of several ways, from blatantly using the "keys" to the state's system of election administration to support or enable the election of candidates from one's own political party, to pushing for facially neutral election reforms that are known or likely to have the effect of making it easier for voters of one political party to vote. The biased actions could come at the request of a Secretary's own party, or could be independent actions that a Secretary takes in furtherance of their own individual bias. Perceived bias is, of course, based primarily on the public's perception that actual bias is occurring. It is most likely the result of accusations that a state's chief election official is somehow using their office to promote the success of their own political party, which could emerge in media reports, litigation, or allegations from other political leaders. And while actual bias has a marked effect on the purity of the electoral process, the effect that perceived bias may have on voters' confidence in the process make it nearly as harmful.

Secretaries of State and Partisan Activities

Other than the infamous examples of Harris and Blackwell, there are a handful of recent examples of Democratic and Republican Secretaries of State articulating their support for certain candidates in elections they are charged with overseeing. Arizona Secretary of State Jan Brewer proudly served as the Arizona chair of then-President George Bush's re-election campaign. Michigan Secretary of State Terri Lynn Land has touted her partisan ties on the Michigan Secretary of State website, with a biography that previously described her as a "longtime Republican

8 See, e.g., Hasen, *supra* note 5; Daniel P. Tokaji, *Early Returns on Election Reform: Discretion, Disenfranchisement, and the Help America Vote Act*, 73 Geo. Wash. L. Rev. 1206 (2005).

activist" beginning with her 1978 stint as one of the "youngest attendees at the 1978 Republican State Convention." Her official biography also notes that in 2004, she "served as Michigan Co-Chair for the Bush-Cheney 2004 reelection campaign, where she brought her trademark enthusiasm and grassroots activism to the campaign trail."

Despite a trend away from Secretaries making such bold endorsements,[9] several continued to be involved in campaigns for candidates in elections that they were overseeing in 2008. Secretaries in Indiana, Arizona, Arkansas, and Rhode Island endorsed candidates in the presidential primaries.[10] Arizona Secretary Brewer campaigned for John McCain, and Indiana Secretary Todd Rokita served as co-chair of Presidential Candidate Mitt Romney's Indiana finance committee. Rhode Island Secretary Ralph Mollis and Arkansas Secretary Charlie Daniels both endorsed Hillary Clinton in their state's Democratic primary.

Endorsements may reveal a Secretary's personal preference for a candidate, but of course, it does not automatically follow that the Secretary is going to use their office to do anything untoward to influence the results of the election. Whether a Secretary ultimately is acting on their individual biases is most often left to innuendo and accusations, or in inferences made in litigation brought by opposing political parties.

In 2004, for example, amidst Democrats' criticism of Ohio's Republican Secretary Blackwell, Democratic Secretaries in New Mexico and Iowa were under fire from allegations from Republican officials due to their treatment of provisional ballots.[11] And in 2005, then-California Secretary Kevin Shelley was forced to resign after a report from the state's auditor suggested that he used federal money received under the Help America Vote Act to support Democratic party activities.[12]

In 2008, Georgia Secretary of State Karen Handel, the state's first Republican Secretary of State and former official in the Bush–Quayle White House, was accused of "manipulating state politics for the GOP" by several newspapers—one described Handel as "part of a long-range plan by Republicans to use the secretary of state's office to solidify and expand their hold on Georgia politics."[13] At the heart of the stories were accusations that Handel was trying to remove Democratic

---

9 Prah, Pamela, *State Election Officials Steer Neutral in 2008*, Stateline.org, Aug. 22, 2007, http://www.stateline.org/live/details/story?contentId=234017 (accessed July 22, 2009).

10 Christian M. Sande, *Where Perception Meets Reality: The Elusive Goal of Impartial Election Oversight*, 34 Wm. Mitchell L. Rev. 729 (2008).

11 Hasen, *supra* note 5.

12 California State Auditor, *Office of the Secretary of State: Clear and Appropriate Direction Is Lacking in Its Implementation of the Federal Help America Vote Act*, http://www.bsa.ca.gov/pdfs/reports/2004-139.pdf (accessed July 22, 2009).

13 Bill Shipp, *Handel Manipulating State Politics for GOP*, Athens Banner Herald, Aug. 17, 2008, http://onlineathens.com/stories/081708/opinion_2008081700425.shtml (accessed July 22, 2009).

candidates from various races, based on the argument that they didn't meet various qualifications. One account involved a judge overturning Handel's decision to disqualify a candidate in the Democratic primary for a seat on the Public Service Commission. Handel had removed the candidate from the ballot on the grounds that he did not meet the residency requirements to run for the seat. State law, she argued, requires candidates for that position to live in their district for the twelve months prior to an election, even though they are elected statewide.

A second account occurred in June 2008: a Republican state senator who was running for re-election withdrew from the race. While state law required Handel to accept new candidates for the position under such circumstances, she only accepted new candidate applications from Republican candidates. Handel was also accused of "fighting tooth and nail" to allow a Republican State Representative, Mike Jacobs, to run unopposed by deeming both his Democratic opponent and an independent candidate ineligible to run. And in October 2008, various media outlets argued that Handel was subjecting voter registration cards to overly-excessive background checks.[14]

Handel responded to all of these claims in an editorial in Georgia's largest paper, the Atlanta Journal Constitution. She claimed that the focus of her work was on "efforts to uphold Georgia's election laws" and resisting "the demands of partisan elected officials and special interest groups."[15] She argued that all of her actions were based on her interpretations of existing election law, noting in particular that her voter registration verification process was "required by federal law and was upheld by U.S. District Court."

Secretaries of State and "Partisan" Reforms

A Secretary's work to advance certain reforms or changes to their state's election code may also invite suspicions that they are actually working to make it easier for their party's voters to turn out on Election Day. Iowa Secretary Michael Mauro and New Hampshire Secretary Bill Gardner both championed an effort to successfully enact Election Day Registration in their respective states. Their actions invited questions over whether they were using their positions to advance reforms that would make it easier for Democrats to register to vote. But at least in Iowa, nearly every eligible citizen—Democrats and Republicans—was already registered. Instead, Mauro's goal was to ensure that "everybody [was] allowed to participate." In his view, by allowing individuals to register and vote on Election Day, the state was simply eliminating the need for any voter to cast a provisional ballot in the rare scenario that they arrived to vote and were accidentally not on the books.

---

14 *GOP wants to protect right to vote—for right people*, Atl. Jnl. Const., Nov. 12, 2008, http://www.ajc.com/opinion/content/opinion/tucker/stories/2008/11/12/tucked_1112.html (accessed July 22, 2009).

15 Karen Handel, *Voters the Real Winners in Recent Election*, Atl. Jnl. Const. Nov. 17, 2008.

And in 1993, Gardner's championing of Election Day Registration in New Hampshire was not in an effort to further a policy priority of the Democratic Party. His actual motivation was to ensure that his state was exempt from the requirements of the newly enacted National Voter Registration Act. Yet the Democratic chairman at the time accused Gardner of pushing a policy that would help Republicans get elected in higher numbers.

And in the 1994 elections, the Democratic chairman was partially correct. The first election in which voters were permitted to register and vote on the same day was, as Gardner recalls, "a big Republican sweep." Voters supported GOP candidates in such large numbers that they elected only Republicans to serve in the entire New Hampshire congressional delegation. And in retrospect, to Gardner, Election Day Registration "wasn't a good bill for Democrats." But he reasons, "that's the sign of good legislation, fair legislation" because "what may be helpful to one side currently, may either backfire or change over time as … unintended consequences come to life later."

Indiana Secretary Todd Rokita has come under similar fire for his role in championing additional photo identification requirements for voters in his state. His advocacy for such reforms was, in his words, his "claim to fame." Support for photo identification requirements generally breaks down along party lines, with Republicans typically favoring the requirement of voters to produce identification, and Democrats typically arguing that such requirements make it more difficult for low-income and elderly voters to participate in elections.

But did Rokita advocate for photo identification for Indiana voters to suppress the vote of poor, or elderly, or voters of color, who may vote Democratic and are less likely to possess photo identification? In Rokita's view, he was elected on a promise to enact the requirement, after receiving the Republican party's nomination by meeting with party delegates who voiced their concern that "people are cheating" the process. Rokita claims that he didn't expect the policy to be partisan, since polls showed that "80% of the country was in favor of showing some kind of identification." But, he reasoned, "we're in this era of distrust and this country is so evenly divided for some reason. So any move you make it seems like you're making half the people angry."

Secretaries of State and Partisan Litigation

Partisan bias can also be suspected or inferred when political parties sue a sitting Secretary or otherwise force a Secretary to take a stand for or against the legal position of a political party. This then leads to accusations or suspicions that a Secretary is working on behalf or at the request of or defending the opposing political party. Election related litigation is a relatively new phenomenon—election law professor Richard Hasen estimates that from 1996 to 1999, the average number of election challenge lawsuits was just under 100 per year. But in the four years following the 2000 presidential election, that number jumped to an average of just over 250 lawsuits per year.[16]

One of the most significant recent cases emerged out of new photo identification requirements for voters in Indiana, where the Democratic Party sued the Republican Secretary of State to block the enforcement of the law. In *Indiana Democratic Party v. Todd Rokita*, the United States Supreme Court ultimately upheld the requirement, which Rokita vigorously defended, seemingly allying himself either against one political party (the Democrats) or in support of his own Republican party. After the ruling was issued in April 2008, Rokita issued a statement applauding the decision as a victory in "the national battle for voter protection and state's rights."[17]

Similar litigation emerged in Georgia, in which the Georgia Democratic Party sought to block Republican Secretary Karen Handel from enforcing the state's photo identification requirement. In response to the lawsuit, Handel issued a statement saying she was "truly dismayed by this latest legal maneuver on the part of those opposed to Georgia's common-sense photo ID law." Like Rokita, Handel vigorously and successfully fought off the lawsuit, while accusing the Democratic Party of being "more concerned with disrupting the elections process than with the security of the process."[18] In response, a Georgia Democratic Party spokesperson accused Handel of "responding like a partisan despite being the elected official whose job is to oversee fair elections."[19]

When asked about the partisan allegations, Handel reasoned: "I think we live in a time when presidential elections particularly, they are very close in the United States right now. And so people look for whatever edge that they can get." Handel laments that "the volume of litigation is overwhelming. And why? Because it has become a campaign tactic." Similarly, she noted, people "trying to call out a Secretary of State, has become a campaign tactic and a rally cry for one candidate or another if he or she doesn't get a favorable ruling on their position from a Secretary of State. [They assume that] it can't possibly be because that Secretary was following the law, it had to be because he or she was partisan."

Apart from accusations and innuendo that Secretaries are acting in a biased fashion when they defend existing legislation against legal attacks from opposing political parties, Secretaries can similarly be accused of being disloyal to their own party if they act in a way that harms their party's candidate or policy. One Secretary admitted that he gets "flack behind the scenes" from his own party, telling him "you should have done that, you should have done this, you should have helped us out."

---

16 Hasen, *supra* note 5.

17 *U.S. Supreme Court Upholds Indiana's Voter ID Law: Indiana Secretary of State Todd Rokita Lauds Decision*, Indiana Secretary of State, April 28, 2008, http://www.in.gov/sos/press/2008/042808.html.

18 Rhonda Cook, *Handel Blasts Move to Halt Voter ID for July 15*, July 3, 2008, http://www.ajc.com/metro/content/metro/stories/2008/07/03/voter_id.html.

19 Steve Visser, *Georgia Democrats Sue Over Voter ID Law*, Atl. Jnl. Const. May 29, 2008, http://www.ajc.com/news/content/metro/stories/2008/05/29/voter_id_lawsuit.html.

If they refuse, they run the risk that their own party may publicly turn against them. In June 2008, Maine Secretary of State Matt Dunlap determined that an independent candidate for U.S. Senate, Herbert Hoffman, could remain on the ballot, despite allegations that Hoffman had violated the rules for gathering nominating petition signatures. Maine Democratic Party sued Dunlap, worried that Hoffman, a former Democrat running as an independent, could take votes away from their candidate.

The suit against Dunlap, a Democrat, carried with it a question of Dunlap's loyalty to the political party that helped him get elected. But Dunlap defended his decision to keep Hoffman on the ballot, reasoning:

> "My role is to protect the voter and stand up for the rights of the voter. And that is not a partisan task. And you talk to any Secretary of State, whether they are Republican or Democrat, and they'll tell you the same thing. Yes, I'm a Democrat but my viewpoint is that the way that I best serve the interests of my party is to do the right thing, regardless of what their temporal desires are to get someone off a ballot or stop an initiative in its tracks. Because that sets a precedent. Because somewhere down the road, it's going to be our guy that's in that position, and they're going to look back on what we did. They'll say what's good for the goose is good for the gander. So if you screw them now, you're at your own peril down the road."

Noting his decision led to threats from his own party to field candidates to run against him, Dunlap insisted:

> "Your political enemies will come to you and lay a plea for justice at your feet. And how you behave at that moment, even if no one sees it, nobody ever knows the difference, it really quantifies whether you are worthy of the public trust or deserving of the public scorn."

Towards Impartiality: The State Secretary of State as a Nonpartisan or Appointed Position

Regardless of whether Secretaries of State are actually working to "swing" elections or otherwise alter the electoral playing field to support their party, the effect of such allegations and innuendos on voter confidence is marked. In the days leading up to the November 2004 election, several polls revealed that many voters questioned the fairness of the election process. A New York Times poll revealed that only a third of respondents believed their vote would be counted, and a Rasmussen Poll estimated that nearly 60 percent of Americans were concerned that the 2004 election would lead to another "Florida-style mess."[20] Four years later, a CBS News/New York Times poll in October 2008 found that 35 percent

20 Sande, *supra* note 10.

of all voters were concerned their vote would not be counted in the upcoming election, and that 60 percent of African Americans surveyed were concerned their vote would not be counted.[21]

In response to this impact on voter confidence, experts and observers have surmised that making the position of a state's chief elections official nonpartisan or appointed would go a long ways towards removing concerns of bias—real or perceived—in how Secretaries operate. In the forefront of those calling for these changes is Professor Rick Hasen, a longtime election law expert who has published extensively in support of nonpartisan election administration. Reasoning that "the people running our elections should not have a vested interest in their outcome," Hasen argues that

> even if [a partisan] election administrator makes a principled decision … that coincides with the interests of his or her party's candidates, opponents in today's highly charged partisan atmosphere will naturally accuse the official of bias. Even worse, an election administrator who makes a principled decision that contradicts the interests of his or her party will be accused of not being sufficiently loyal to the party. The appearance of corruption … is apparent and unavoidable.[22]

Hasen's solution is to create a "cadre of individuals" whose allegiance "is to the integrity of the process itself, and not to any particular electoral outcome." Hasen argues that the state's chief election official should be "nominated by the governor and approved by a large supermajority of the state legislature (say a 75% vote), insuring that only a consensus candidate who is seen as above politics will gain enough bipartisan support to be awarded the position." The official's appointment should be "a long term without the possibility of reappointment," removable only by the legislature "under the rules for impeaching a state executive" and guaranteed a certain budget level so as to isolate the office from the need to depend on legislators for funding.[23]

Apart from the political difficulties of instituting Hasen's proposal—it would require significant amendments to a state's constitution and the support of political party leaders who are invested in the current process—there are several criticisms that emerged in my own conversations with Secretaries of State. Though most agreed with Hasen's view that impartiality was crucial for a state's chief election official, nearly every Secretary emphasized that such a proposal assumes first that there are a multitude of individuals capable of filling the role who have no current or prior affiliation with any political party (an idea that Oregon Secretary of State Bill Bradbury called "baloney" and "complete B.S."). Indiana Secretary Rokita,

21 CBS News/New York Times Poll, CBS News, Oct. 30, 2008, http://www.cbsnews.com/htdocs/pdf/Oct08e-all.pdf, at page 8.

22 Hasen, *supra* note 5.

23 *Id.* at 985.

himself no stranger to accusations of partisan bias, reasoned: "To find a quote unquote nonpartisan is to find someone in a bubble. And is that the kind of person that you want running the show?"

Vermont Secretary Deborah Markowitz said simply, "I don't think there is such a thing [as a nonpartisan]. Do you know anyone who is nonpartisan? Everyone [involved in the political arena] has an opinion on who they are going to vote for for president." Washington Secretary of State Sam Reed remarked, "in my experience working with non-party city councilmen and nonpartisan mayors, some of them are the most partisan people I know." Secretary Bradbury pointed to two statewide nonpartisan positions in Oregon—the Superintendent of Public Instruction and the Commissioner of Labor, both of whom were active Democratic leaders in the Oregon legislature prior to their selection. As Bradbury remarked: "Non-partisan? I don't think so."

Alabama Secretary of State Beth Chapman agreed that "politics are going to always be in politics." She noted that

> "even appointing a Secretary of State, do I think that that person's going to have some political background or some life experience that would sway them one way or another? Yes! Just like with Judges, you can have them appointed all day long but they still have philosophies that either align them as a conservative or a liberal or a Republican or a Democrat."

In addition, most Secretaries cautioned that making the position appointed, or elected in a nonpartisan fashion, would more likely cause an individual to simply mask their party affiliation behind a cloak of nonpartisanship, drastically altering the ability of voters to hold accountable the individuals who are running elections in their state. Vermont Secretary Markowitz opined: "I think in our elections system we need to have transparency and accountability. And, a nonpartisan Secretary of State [is] not transparent." Secretary Bradbury reasoned similarly that a requirement for Secretaries to run as nonpartisan "den[ies]voters access to really critical information that they might want to know about those various candidates." He emphasized "I'm a Democrat and I make no bones about it. I'm a Democrat, and that means that every person in this state can evaluate what I do, I do with a very clear understanding of where I am coming from. I want people to know who I am." Thus making the position nonpartisan, in Nebraska Secretary of State John Gale's view, "may put the politics into the back room, but it doesn't take it out of politics."

Rokita took the accountability argument a few steps further, emphasizing the importance of voters being able to hold their election officials accountable at the ballot box as preferable to allowing a governor or legislature or other entity to appoint an individual or board. Rokita declared: "If this country is to stay free, it has to stay in the people's hands. And that's from the chief election administrator all the way down to the poll worker." South Dakota Secretary of State Chris Nelson surmised that "everyday [I] wake up I am accountable for every single person in my state. And not just a governor, not just the legislature, but every single person in the state, and as I talk to people, people will call me if they have an issue about something and I'll tell them right up front 'you're my boss.' Everyday I get up and I work for every one of these people." Kansas Secretary of State Ron Thornburgh gives

> "credit to the voters of the state of Kansas. If I were to become partisan, I guarantee you they would remove me in a heartbeat. And I think in particular it becomes: who are we responsible to report to? Who do we report to? I think from a systematic point of view though it's better to be reliant upon the voters than it is to be reliant on a single entity like a governor or even a board. Because the constituency is too small and the opportunity to sway is too great."

And in the view of North Dakota Secretary Al Jaeger: "I have to answer to the voters directly, I am accountable, I am responsible. Regardless of which party I belong to." Secretary Chapman concurred:

> "I like people electing their leaders because I think that holds me accountable. Someone just asked me who audits me and I said you do, every four years. I answer to all people, I don't answer to one man or one woman in a closed door office who can call me in and put pressure on me to make a decision based upon what they think is right."

Thus the reality is that any entity—individual or board, appointee or elected official—who could run elections is beholden to someone. The question is who should they be beholden to? A Governor? A Governor and a legislature, as Hasen suggests? Or the voters? In the view of Iowa Secretary Michael Mauro:

> "If I'm doing the job as an appointed official, I already [am conflicted] right at the beginning because the first time they ask me to [do] something that I don't agree with, I'm now in conflict with my boss. And [as an elected official], the only boss I have now is the citizens of Iowa."

Louisiana Secretary Jay Dardenne said simply, "I'm not appointed. I don't serve at anyone's pleasure. I serve the people."

Towards Accountability: The Voter's Role in Ensuring an Impartial Secretary of State

What immediately became clear through my research and conversations with various Secretaries was the tremendous power of voters to provide the ultimate "check" on the neutrality of their election officials. Not only did the Secretaries by and large respect that accountability, many revered it. For elections to remain pure, fair, and free under the oversight of partisan elected officials, the voters' accountability power must be combined with a mandate that the officials act in an impartial and apolitical manner.

For what most Secretaries said may be true. In most situations it is difficult and rare to be able to elect, appoint, or even find an individual who is at once qualified and willing to serve as the state's chief election official and also truly has no ties to any political party. But voters can mandate that Secretaries act in an impartial and unbiased manner in overseeing elections.

How would voters do this? Well, it may be obvious: voters can refuse to re-elect or can otherwise criticize and condemn Secretaries who endorse candidates in elections they are overseeing or who are involved in fundraisers for political parties or their candidates. But those actions would still not capture many of the other allegations of bias and partisanship that afflict a state's chief election official, such as legal interpretations and policy reforms that they tout. Such neutral actions with potential partisan implications were at the heart of many of the accusations that surrounded Harris in 2000 and Blackwell in 2004. How are voters to review or evaluate the impartiality of Secretaries beyond asking whether they endorse or oppose or support partisan candidates or issues?

One option is simply to demand substantive balance. Modern election reforms can usually be classified in one of two ways: they seek either to primarily promote access to participation, or they seek to protect the integrity of the process and accuracy of the outcomes. This access/integrity dichotomy typically falls, for various reasons, along partisan lines, with Democrats generally favoring policies that promote access and Republicans emphasizing policies that promote integrity.[24]

What's more, often times reforms that advance one of those goals—such as Election Day Registration, which promotes access to participation—are seen by critics, who argue that it enables voter impersonation fraud, as potentially harming the goals of protecting the integrity of the process and accuracy of the outcomes. Photo identification is another example. Critics argue that identification requirements reduce voter participation, while advocates insist that it is necessary to protect the integrity of the ballot box.

Balance, then, comes from demanding that any action an election official takes to promote one interest (access) be balanced with an action to promote the opposing interest (integrity). Efforts to advocate for voter identification or limits on voter registration drives—designed to protect the integrity of elections against fraud or other types of malfeasance—should be coupled with efforts to widen the avenues available for one to cast their ballot—such as allowing voters to register on Election Day, vote early, or vote absentee with no excuse.

---

24 Richard Hasen, *The Untimely Death of Bush v. Gore*, 60 Stanford L. Rev. 1 (2007); Daniel P. Tokaji, *Leave It to the Lower Courts: On Judicial Intervention in Election Administration*, 68 Ohio St. L.J. (2007) at 1207 ("For the most part, Democrats advocated expanded access that would enhance equality, while Republicans advocated tougher antifraud measures that would enhance integrity").

The United States Congress recognized and endorsed this balance when it enacted the National Voter Registration Act in 1993. The NVRA's stated purpose was to both "establish procedures that will increase the number of eligible citizens who register to vote in elections" and "protect the integrity of the electoral process; and … ensure that accurate and current voter registration rolls are maintained."[25] And a review of the actions and pledges of Secretaries serving in 2008 and 2009 indicates that many Secretaries are already aware of the importance, not only of not endorsing or otherwise supporting candidates or parties, but also of maintaining this balance of promoting access and integrity in the democratic process.

Secretaries of State and Efforts to be Impartial

In the years following the 2000 election, a handful of states enacted legislation requiring that their chief election official remain neutral in all state and federal races. Louisiana Secretary Jay Dardenne sponsored such a law in his state when he was serving in the state legislature. Dardenne's law specifically "prohibit[ed] a Secretary from being involved in any political race except his own." Dardenne explained his support for the policy as promoting voter confidence and protecting perceptions of fairness "because when your legislature says that the Secretary of State cannot be involved in partisan politics it certainly throttles any efforts an otherwise partisan secretary may want to engage in." As Secretary, Dardenne complies with his law by making an effort to

> "foster a sense that we are operating this office in a nonpartisan way. Because obviously elections are so partisan and it creates such divisiveness within a state or between parties, it's very important to me to conduct this office in a way that was going to be perceived as playing it right down the middle and to do what was appropriate and to ensure fairness and the integrity of the electoral process."

But as Christian Sande, a former candidate for Minnesota Secretary of State notes, an ethics code alone "cannot eliminate an individual's partisanship." Sande describes how in Colorado, despite a policy that barred him from "publicly endorsing or working for a political candidate, political party, or statewide ballot initiative, former Colorado Secretary of State Michael Coffman continued to be an "active Republican," speaking at various Republican party gatherings and eventually winning a seat in the U.S. House of Representatives.[26]

Dardenne's championing of an ethics code in Louisiana stemmed more from his own individual commitment to impartiality. This commitment was echoed by several other Secretaries of State, many of whom emphasized that, whether elected as a Democrat or Republican, under a legal mandate of impartiality or not, voters have the power to verify ongoing impartiality by evaluating and electing

25 42 U.S.C. 1973gg(b).

26 Sande, *supra* note 10.

individual candidates with a commitment to ensuring the office operates free from partisanship. And many Secretaries pointed to their knowledge of or commitment to the law as a helpful bellwether to indicate an individual's dedication to fairness. As Secretary Markowitz put it—are the individuals serving as a state's chief election official "substantive" or "political?" Markowitz pointed to her background as a municipal attorney as evidence that she was "more substance than politics." Secretary Handel agreed, emphasizing that "the most important thing" is for Secretaries "to make decisions based off of the law, in the best interest of the voters and democracy. And then, deal with the politics of the decision after the fact. And so as long as you keep your priorities straight that it is the law, the voters, and democracy, then you can always deal with the other part of it."

It is also not uncommon for Secretaries on both sides of the political spectrum to proudly decline any involvement in partisan campaigns. New Hampshire Secretary Bill Gardner has never attended a fundraiser, candidate event, nor has he ever endorsed a candidate. After receiving the endorsement from the Rhode Island Secretary of State, a Hillary Clinton campaign official made a similar endorsement request to Maine Secretary Matt Dunlap, to which he said, simply "I can't. I'm a chief elections officer." And Nebraska Secretary John Gale has

> "had statewide campaigns come to me and say 'gosh we'd sure like to have you on our honorary committee,' and I would have to say no! I won't endorse anybody. I will not give campaign advice, I will not go sit in on campaign meetings, I will not allow anybody to come into my office and talk about a campaign."

At the same time, Gale realistically admits

> "as a partisan office holder I have to be sensitive to be involved in politics. I can't just divorce myself from politics. So, I do go speak to county republican central committees, I attend our state convention, and I usually act as a Master of Ceremony for some of those events. But I don't see that as in any way conflicting with my duties as chief election officer, as long as I maintain this balance within my office and so long as I don't get involved in any way in any of the campaigns."

Nevada Secretary Ross Miller simply tries "as much as I can to stay out of the political fray" by not endorsing "any presidential candidates, even though I had a lot of pressure to do so" because Nevada was an early caucus state during the presidential primaries. To Miller, "if you get in a situation where it's a very tight election and you're called upon to make some difficult decisions, you've got to maintain as much objectivity as you possibly can." South Dakota Secretary Chris Nelson similarly described how "candidates and parties will come to us for request" to "shift" a certain way. To Nelson,

> "it doesn't matter which party it is, we're going to tell them no. We're going to go right down the middle, we're going to do it right, and to do it fair. We're not going to tilt the process, we're going to run our campaigns, we're going to have a fair election, and in the end whoever wins we know is justly and properly elected."

Nebraska Secretary John Gale and Vermont Secretary Markowitz take these efforts one step further, and both have selected someone from the opposing party to be their deputy. To Markowitz, a Democrat, having a deputy who is "perceived as a Republican creates a balance." And Gale, a Republican, has kept a Democrat deputy also to ensure that "we've got balance in my office, [and that] we can show transparency and accountability." To Gale,

> "if the deputy for election is the opposite party of the secretary of state it maintains an equity and a balance. We have to serve the public in a way that sustains their confidence in the election process and doing that by having a balanced office in elections is the best way to do that."

Another more visible approach some Secretaries have taken is to make a longstanding, public pledge to serve in an impartial manner. Markowitz estimated that in 2008, all but four or five Secretaries of State have adopted personal policies of not participating in any campaign aside from their own, in order to "make sure that the voters have confidence in the position." California Secretary Debra Bowen is one of the Secretaries who has adopted her own code of ethics, voluntarily, to prohibit herself from "taking a position in a contest in which she is certifying the outcomes." Bowen admits that it hasn't been easy to adhere to that code "because people who you've known a long time and who helped you get elected will say 'Well, I support you, can you support me?' And my answer is always 'No, I can't.' I don't want either bias or the appearance of bias. And if I were to start appearing on campaign stages with candidates and there were a difficult call to be made about election procedures, people would have a right to be skeptical about motivation."

Wyoming Secretary Max Maxfield is another who has proudly pledged complete impartiality, having "made the decision personally, just to add an extra layer of confidence, that I will not endorse, participate, or campaign or support any candidate for the federal offices." Maxfield introduced the policy himself to ensure that voters "have full confidence that I'm objective." And he predicts further that when he is running for re-election himself, his deputy will play a larger role in overseeing the election process to ensure complete impartiality.

Former Oregon Secretary Bill Bradbury has taken a similar pledge to not endorse a candidate or serve on the finance committee or as an officer in any campaign in Oregon where he would be counting the ballots. Bradbury calls this his "Fair and Neutral Election Administration pledge." And he admits to having "mixed feelings about it" because though he says people understand when he declines to offer an endorsement, explaining, "I'm sorry, but I've got to count the votes," difficulties remain. For Bradbury, it was when a lifelong friend was running for the Oregon House of Representatives. Bradbury declined to endorse him, adhering to his pledge, but allowed the candidate to include a quote from Bradbury "saying very glowing things about him" in the candidate's literature. In response to criticism that he broke his pledge, Bradbury "took the family members excuse and it was forgiven."

Conclusion

The curious tension underlying the role of partisanship influence over a Secretary's actions is that most Secretaries run as the nominee of a particular party. This often entails engendering support from one party's leaders, and voters, thus implying some sort of allegiance to that party. And when they arrive into office, voters may expect them to execute their office as though they were unaffiliated with any political party, but those party leaders and supporters who led to their election may expect those Secretaries to further their interests and theirs alone.

The foregoing anecdotes describe Secretaries' efforts to strike that balance. One overall key factor in the effectiveness of those efforts, though, is transparency. Whether Secretaries are individually acting in a partisan fashion, or proudly decrying any efforts to be involved in campaigns, it is crucial that they be transparent in their actions and work to explain any misconception that may arise from their decisions.

Increased transparency then enables the voters to better evaluate the actions of their Secretary of State, and hold them accountable to using the office in a nonpartisan manner. Maine Secretary Dunlap underscored this point, noting that "there is no automatic way to protect your rights unless to be vigilant and to hold your public officials accountable. If the Secretary of State behaves in a partisan manner, and you don't want them to, you get them out of office."

New Hampshire Secretary Bill Gardner agrees, and believes that at the end of the day, "people don't want [this] to be a partisan office. They don't want it to be based on partisanship. And they want the elections to be fair and transparent. Everyone has an equal opportunity to be elected. They want the rules to apply the same way to everyone." Vermont Secretary Markowitz agreed, because "at the end of the day Katherine Harris was not elected to the Senate. At the end of the day Ken Blackwell was perceived as making decisions that had partisan advantage, and he was not elected Governor."

In other words, the power of the voter to protect the office from partisanship prevailed.

Georgia Secretary of State
Karen Handel

First Elected: 2006

Karen Handel made history on January 8, 2007 when she became the first Republican to take office as Secretary of State in Georgia. She gained her political chops serving as a deputy chief of staff under the Bush–Quayle administration. Originally from Texas, Handel became active in the Georgia Republican Party in 2002 when she served as deputy chief of staff to Governor Sonny Perdue. The following year she was elected Chairman of the Fulton County Board of Commissioners.

Handel served as Secretary during the initial implementation of the state's photo identification requirement, which is one of the most stringent in the nation. After years of litigation, the state law mandating that every citizen produce picture identification prior to voting on Election Day went into effect in 2008. And Handel, at the behest of a federal district court, executed a widespread grassroots statewide voter education program targeting every registered voter who did not have a state ID or driver's license in the months leading up to the first election where voters would need to comply with the law.

To Karen Handel, whose intelligence is rivaled only by her warmth, the program was a welcome aspect to her job as Secretary of State. "As a group," she mentioned, "and I say this for Republicans and Democrats, we all take our jobs extremely seriously. And those of us who handle elections, we understand that we've got to be mindful of going the extra mile to be fair and judicious."

Chapter 3
The Secretary and Congressional Oversight

"We are as a group very resistant to [Congressional] intrusion, because we're the ones doing it. We really welcome the support. Good changes are good changes. But a reform for reforms' sake only confuses things."

Maine Secretary of State Matt Dunlap

The first chapter of this book offers a brief overview of the role that Congress and other entities have played in election administration, particularly in the past decade. The role that Congress has played in election administration and oversight has not only grown exponentially in recent years, it has had a marked nationwide effect on the functions of a state's chief elections official. Particularly following the 2002 passage of the Help America Vote Act, Secretaries across the country have uniformly seen their roles altered and their independence limited due to federal legislation. That in and of itself, of course, is not a bad thing. But federal legislation enacted even with the best political intentions can produce side effects that, for better or for worse, significantly alter the actions and abilities of similarly well intentioned state Secretaries of State.

Throughout history, most significantly in 1965 with the passage of the Voting Rights Act and in 2002 with the enactment of the Help America Vote Act, Congress has sought an increased role in ensuring that the fundamental right to vote inherent in the U.S. Constitution is protected and preserved. Congressional oversight over federal elections is rooted in various parts of the U.S. Constitution, including Article I's Spending Clause and Elections Clause, the Fourteenth Amendment's Equal Protection Clause, the Fifteenth Amendment's protections of voting rights regardless of race, the Nineteenth Amendment's protection of voting rights regardless of gender, and the Twenty-Sixth Amendment's protection of voting rights for citizens over the age of eighteen.

But beyond the legal authority of oversight lies the political ramifications for Secretaries of State. Most Secretaries I spoke with appreciated the efforts of Congress to ensure fair elections, but were uncomfortable with what they viewed as a federal assumption of superiority. That sense of superiority, in the view of many state election officials, runs counter to the fact that it is the state Secretaries of State who possess a ground-level view of the election process. And more important, many Secretaries observed that congressional actions, particularly in the past ten years, are rooted in a sense of distrust that state elections officials are capable of and committed to protecting the democratic process.

South Dakota Secretary Chris Nelson, for example, expressed frustration with Congress's efforts to "micromanage what we do." And Wyoming Secretary Max

Maxfield traveled to Washington DC a few months after he took office in 2006 and was "absolutely flabbergasted" to find "the national attitude, by the Congressional members, by some of the national election groups, the jaundiced eye that they had on the ability of the states to conduct their own elections." In Maxfield's view:

> "[W]hat I was seeing, the latest poll from CNN had said that 83 or 85% of the people polled had confidence in their voting systems. And yet the verbage that we were getting in Washington by a couple of Congressman and some of the national press indicated that there was great possibility for nefarious action by Secretaries of State. And I don't know what kind of powers or latitude other Secretaries have but I can assure you it couldn't and wouldn't happen in Wyoming. I guess I was a little shocked that in the last election it seemed like there were a couple of hot spots, and Congress came in and [assumed] there would be a one size fits all solution, and ignored concerns about the erosion of states' rights in conducting their own elections. And that is extremely troubling to me. One Congressman said that the Republic was in jeopardy because of the lack of trust that states could run elections fairly. It just blew me away."

Congressional Oversight from 1965 to 2002

The Voting Rights Act of 1965

The congressional oversight role, though consistently well intentioned, has always been a bit of a thorn in the side of state elections officials. While election administration was almost entirely left to the states for the first roughly 200 years of the American democracy, Congress's involvement in elections took a great leap forward in 1965, with the passage of the Voting Rights Act (VRA). Sections 5 and 203 of the VRA both place specific requirements on a select few jurisdictions that either have a history of discrimination (Section 5), or significant populations of citizens with limited English proficiency (Section 203). With the exception of former Ohio Secretary of State Kenneth Blackwell, who has called the legislation designed to protect the rights of voters of color "draconian",[1] most Secretaries who discussed the law aligned more closely with the views of California Secretary Debra Bowen. Bowen's state must comply with both Section 5's preclearance requirements and Section 203's mandate that certain localities provide translated election materials, and she stated emphatically that "certainly there is nothing in the Voting Rights Act that is anything but helpful."

Of course, no law is perfect. And South Dakota Secretary Chris Nelson in particular expressed his frustrations with the enforcement of provisions in ways that do not match, in his view, the needs of the voters in his state. Since he came

1 Kenneth Blackwell, *Obama Justice*, The Washington Times, Dec. 31, 2008, http://washingtontimes.com/news/2008/dec/31/obama-justice/.

to the office in 2002, Nelson has specifically grappled with complying with both Sections 5 and 203 of the VRA. When he learned that under Section 5, South Dakota was required to seek approval from the U.S. Justice Department for any election law changes—something the state had failed to do in seventeen years, Nelson "personally prepared the pre-clearance submissions for that seventeen year period, 3,048 changes, every single one of which were pre-cleared." Nelson spent "a tremendous amount of my time on that paperwork chase," to get the state in compliance with the provision that his predecessors had ignored for nearly two decades, and questioned whether the time spent on addressing the backlog would have been better spent on protecting current voters' needs.

Nelson also has had some unique experiences with Section 203 of the VRA, which requires that states or local jurisdictions with a certain percentage of citizens of Spanish, Native American, Alaska Native, or Asian descent who fall under the national literacy rate provide translated election materials for those populations. South Dakota's Native American population is large enough and has a low enough literacy rate to require compliance with Section 203, though in Nelson's view the population is shrinking and may have fallen under the threshold in recent years (the population threshold has not been updated since the 2000 Census, but will be updated in 2010). The population that is covered under Section 203 speaks Lakota, which is an unwritten language and requires oral translation with the AutoMARK machines that were provided to states via the Help America Vote Act.

Yet in Nelson's observation, it is elderly voters who are in the greatest need of these translations, and those voters "are not going to sit down at an AutoMARK machine, and put headphones on, and try to navigate through the ballot. It's just not going to happen." And because the AutoMARK machines are not programmed with Lakota, the specific language, the Secretary of State's office must manually program the machines with volunteer translators. The process was, in Nelson's words, "very difficult, very cumbersome, very tough to program, and it's frankly the toughest part of what we do in the whole election process." There may be other more cost efficient ways to comply with Section 203 in South Dakota, such as collaborating with community groups to recruit bilingual poll workers. But the Justice Department's enforcement of the provision led to the AutoMARK solution, even if it wasn't, in Nelson's view, the most appropriate or effective application of Section 203 for the local jurisdiction.

The 1993 National Voter Registration Act

Though the enforcement of the provisions of the VRA may frustrate some Secretaries—a 1970s publication from the National Association of Secretaries of State (NASS) describes the "offense" some members of the Association took to "the federal government's encroachment on states' rights in election procedures"[2]—its

2 National Association of Secretaries of State, *Pillars of Public Service: A History of NASS*, http://nass.org/index.php?option=com_docman&task=doc_download&gid=3 (accessed Dec. 11, 2008).

impact on protecting voters' rights across the country was sufficient to keep it as the sole significant piece of federal legislation addressing election administration for thirty years. Throughout that time span, several Secretaries and NASS began focusing for the first time on improving voter education efforts. In the months leading up to the 1980 presidential election, NASS formed a special committee that worked with the Ad Council to develop the organization's first significant Get Out the Vote campaign.[3]

A few cycles later, in 1988, NASS built on its previous work and established a "Task Force on Barriers to Voting" to urge enactment of legislation to expand opportunities for voter registration. In the years that followed the creation of the task force, several Secretaries of State, including former Michigan Secretary Richard Austin and former Washington Secretary Ralph Munro, consulted and worked with members of Congress to craft legislation to expand and promote registration opportunities for voters throughout the country.[4] Out of those discussions emerged a second significant piece of congressional oversight legislation addressing election administration: the National Voter Registration Act (NVRA).

The NVRA required all states, with some exceptions, to expand voter registration opportunities for eligible citizens. It specifically required states to provide its citizens with the opportunity to register by mail, at any offices that provide public assistance or services to citizens with disabilities, or when they apply for or renew their driver's license.[5] The NVRA also requires that states notify registration applicants if their voter registration was rejected or accepted, and dictates the parameters around when states may remove voters from registration lists (e.g., voters cannot be removed within ninety days of an election). It also exempts from its mandates any state that, as of the date of its enactment in 1993, allows voters to register to vote on Election Day (i.e., Election Day or Same Day Registration).

That exemption was particularly relevant for election officials in New Hampshire and Idaho, who balked at the new law's requirements and conferred on ways to squirm out of coverage. New Hampshire Secretary Bill Gardner was most concerned that the NVRA would actually decrease voter turnout by making it easier to register and vote. He recalls:

> "I said at the time that it's going to decrease the turnout in the country. I was like a fool to everybody. They said, 'This is crazy! How can you say this!' And I said if you cheapen the process, if you cheapen the vote, it becomes less valuable to the average person and it becomes easier for them not to bother to participate. And no one really got that. They said this is going to help turnout [increase]. People thought it was the government's fault that people weren't voting because we don't make it easy enough to register. [And so they thought,] '[W]e're going to do this and we'll get a bigger turnout.'"

3 *Id.* at 26.

4 *Id.*

5 National Voter Registration Act, 42 U.S.C. § 1973gg-3 to -5 (1993).

Gardner's concerns went beyond the potential reduction in turnout. He believed, and still does, that enabling mail in voter registration was a recipe for chaos with the voter registration system, leading to "part time agencies doing registration that aren't going to be familiar with it, and that may lose registration forms." Gardner did not want to have "outside groups doing registration drives" in New Hampshire, and stated his preference for allowing in person voter registration on Election Day as a way to minimize the potential for fraud because "people are much less likely to commit fraud if they have to do it in person." And Gardner maintains that part of the chaos and confusion that surrounded the 2000 presidential election in Florida "was the result of the [NVRA]. Because people were going in to vote and they were told they weren't on the list, they couldn't vote, and they were sent home. And they said, 'I registered up at Disney World' And election officials said in response, 'well we didn't get anything, we can't help you.' And the voters were sent home without being able to vote."

Former President Bill Clinton signed the NVRA into effect in May 1993. To ensure that his concerns about the negative impact of the legislation did not extend to his state of New Hampshire, Gardner worked with the state legislature to enact Election Day Registration, making it retroactive to the day that Congress enacted the NVRA. "The only way out," Gardner recalls, "was to have Election Day registration" on the day the NVRA was enacted. "So after the bill passed, I asked the legislature to pass Election Day registration and make it retroactive to the day that Congress passed the NVRA." The state of Idaho followed Gardner's lead, with then-Idaho Secretary Pete Cenarrusa calling Gardner to ask for a copy of the New Hampshire Election Day registration statute. Idaho subsequently enacted an identical version of the law to skirt NVRA coverage. Current Idaho Secretary Ben Ysursa recalled that Gardner's actions and the passage of the NVRA were "an absolute catalyst for us to go to Election Day Registration."

There had yet to be a federal election in which the NVRA applied, and Gardner reasoned that so long as Election Day Registration was in place by the federal election in November 1994, the state would have complied with the exemption. But not everyone agreed. Gardner eventually worked to get an amendment to the NVRA that specifically exempted New Hampshire from coverage.[6]

A New Era of Oversight: The Help America Vote Act of 2002

A publication of the National Association of Secretaries of State referred to the 2000 election as marking "the beginning of a reform process that would change the way elections are conducted in America."[7] Indeed, less than ten years had gone by after the NVRA was passed before the 2000 presidential election threw the election administration world upside down.

6 42 U.S.C. § 1973gg-2(b) (1996).

7 NASS, *supra* note 2, at 33.

Vermont Secretary Deborah Markowitz recalls how "living through the 2000 elections was really, really surprising." Until then, overseeing election administration had been "a fairly mundane aspect" of her work as Secretary of State. To Markowitz, "the fact that a Secretary of State's failure of leadership … really made the difference in the presidential race … led to monumental changes." Markowitz believed that what occurred in Florida in the 2000 presidential election might have easily happened in many other states. She noted that

> "what was even more surprising to me was finding out from my peers after this 2000 election, when we met in February that many of them felt like but for the Grace of God it could've happened in their state. … I found that routinely states tolerated the loss of a hundred thousand votes or more in those lever machines. That was shocking to me, that there was a tolerance in other places of that kind of failure."

Shortly after the 2000 presidential election, the University of Virginia's Miller Center of Public Affairs and the Century Foundation convened a National Commission on Federal Election Reform, dubbed the "Carter-Ford" Commission because it was jointly chaired by former Presidents Jimmy Carter and Gerald Ford. The Commission was comprised of thirteen distinguished government officials, including former Senator Daniel Patrick Moynihan and New Mexico Governor Bill Richardson. None of the Commission members had ever served as state Secretaries of State or in any capacity as a statewide election administrator.[8] The Commission, however, did convene several hearings in the wake of the 2000 election, during which a handful of Secretaries of State, including then-Arkansas Secretary Sharon Priest, then-Georgia Secretary Cathy Cox, then-California Secretary Bill Jones, and then-Oregon Secretary Bill Bradbury, presented testimony on election administration issues arising in their respective states.

The Commission issued a report in August 2001 that included several recommendations for national reforms, including the implementation of statewide voter registration databases and providing provisional ballots for voters whose eligibility to vote is unclear when they arrive at a polling place.[9] The report also recommended that the federal government provide funding to improve election technologies and suggested the creation of a new federal agency, the "Election Administration Commission," to "a) develop federal voting system standards in consultation with state and local election administrators; b) oversee the implementation of these standards; c) maintain a national clearinghouse of information on best practices in election administration; and d) administer the limited federal assistance program to the states." The Commission's report also

8 *To Ensure Pride and Confidence in the Electoral Process*, The National Commission on Election Reform, Aug. 2001, http://www.reformelections.org/ncfer.asp.

9 *Id.* The report's recommendations, published August 2001, can be found at: http://www.tcf.org/Publications/ElectionReform/NCFER/tapc1-15.pdf.

emphasized repeatedly that Congress should set minimum thresholds and standards for the states while providing funding for necessary improvements, but should leave the details of various improvements to the respective states.

Enter the Help America Vote Act of 2002 (HAVA).[10] Among its several provisions was the granting of several million dollars to states to upgrade their voting equipment and centralize their voter registration lists into one statewide database. HAVA also created the first federal identification requirement for voters, requiring all first time voters who register by mail (as they now could do, thanks to the NVRA), to vote in person in their first election and to provide some form of acceptable identification when they arrive at the polls to vote. HAVA also allowed any voter who is not found on the registration list when they appear to vote to cast a provisional ballot,[11] which presumably would be counted at a later time if the voter is able to prove they were legally able to cast a ballot in that election.

Despite the absence of their presence on the Carter-Ford Commission, various Secretaries of State, primarily at the behest of and in coordination with NASS, did play a role in the development of the legislation. In the weeks following Election Day, then-Arkansas Secretary of State Sharon Priest, NASS president at the time, convened a bipartisan task force of Secretaries and other election administration experts from around the country. The task force worked to involve several state election administrators in developing a list of recommended election reforms in response to the Florida kerfuffle. Priest emphasized the importance of "bring[ing] together state election administrators who understand our voting process and its flaws," cautioning that the process should be "evolutionary," not "revolutionary."[12]

Kansas Secretary Ron Thornburgh was the elected President of NASS by the time Congress began crafting and debating HAVA in 2001. Working to ensure that the resulting federal reforms were a beneficial response to the 2000 election was, to Thornburgh, one of the "most difficult challenges" of his tenure as Secretary of State. In retrospect, Thornburgh recalled that in 2001 "Congress was prepared to do what Congress always does. When there's a problem, they either do nothing or they overreact. And Congress was highly prepared to overreact. And they were ready to move election responsibility from the county courthouse to Congress. They were moving everything to Washington." But such a drastic overhaul of the country's system of running elections was an overreaction to Thornburgh because, as he told Congress, "in spite of what you may think, the system worked. We had an orderly transfer of power from one political party to the next without the tanks rolling in the streets under a highly contested election. The system worked."

10 Help America Vote Act of 2002, 42 U.S.C.A. 15483 (2006).

11 42 U.S.C.S. § 15483(2)(b)(i) ("an individual who desires to vote in person, but who does not meet the requirements of subparagraph (A)(i), may cast a provisional ballot under section 302(a)").

12 NASS, *supra* note 2, at 36.

But the process of election administration in 2000, Thornburgh admits, "clearly was problematic." The challenge, in Thornburgh's view, was getting Congress "to focus on what the true problems were" and to develop solutions for addressing those specific problems. In Thornburgh's view, "the Supreme Court hit it on the head" in *Bush v. Gore*, concluding that "every voter in every precinct, in every polling place, must be treated uniformly. If we can live up to that standard," said Thornburgh, "then I think we're doing what we need to do." In the end, Thornburgh's work as President of NASS and advocate on behalf of the Secretaries to Congress centered on his view that "the rationale behind federal intervention has to be to provide support and resources and in some cases, guidance. We have to be very careful because one size rarely fits anybody."

In his testimony before both the United States House Committee on House Administration and the U.S. Senate Committee on Commerce, Science, and Transportation, Thornburgh specified: "What works for Los Angeles, California certainly won't work for Leoti, Kansas. This is not a plea to place new technology in every polling place in America. As Senator Nancy Kassebaum Baker told me recently, 'The pencil on a string works very well in Burdick, Kansas, Ron. Don't change it.'"[13] Thornburgh also made a plea for federal funding, testifying that "the hard reality is state and local governments need help funding the best systems to ensure safe, secure and accurate elections. All too often county government has had to face the difficult choice of replacing crumbling roads and bridges, or trying to squeeze another election out of an antiquated system."

Connecticut Secretary Susan Bysiewicz also was involved in the crafting of HAVA, urging her U.S. Senator, Christopher Dodd, a co-sponsor of the legislation in the Senate, to include a provision that enabled states to establish a centralized voter registration system. Other Secretaries, including Vermont Secretary Deb Markowitz, North Dakota Secretary Al Jaeger, and then-Maine Secretary Dan Gwadosky, worked with both congressional leaders from their states and NASS to offer their own perspectives on needed election reforms.

In his speech before the Senate shortly before HAVA's passage, Senator Dodd emphasized his view of both the importance of the legislation and the federal government's deferential role in the oversight of election administration.

> "We, by no means, intend to supplant the traditional role that state and local governments have played administering elections for Federal office," Dodd declared. "But, for the first time, with this legislation, the Congress—the Federal Government—will set basic minimum requirements and provide critical resources for Federal elections [and] will start paying their fair share of the cost of administering elections for Federal office."[14]

13 http://www.kssos.org/other/news_releases/PR_2001/PR_USSenate_Testimony.html (accessed July 1, 2009).

14 148 CONG. REC. S709-03 (daily ed. Feb. 13, 2002) (statement of Sen. Dodd).

Implementation of HAVA: Statewide Voter Registration Database

The new identification and provisional ballot requirements notwithstanding, one of the most significant mandates under HAVA was to require that states receiving federal funds through the legislation to centralize their voter registration databases into one statewide file. Connecticut Secretary Susan Bysiewicz was particularly pleased with the mandate. In her view, prior to the creation of the database, a person in Connecticut "could literally register in Stamford, drive up Interstate 95, register in Norwalk, drive farther up 95, register in Bridgeport, and could then have voted in each of those places and no one would have known the difference."

The Act, which President Bush officially signed into law in October 2002,[15] mandated that each state build a central voter registration database and that it be fully functional statewide by December 31, 2005. Twenty-six states made the deadline, including West Virginia, where, in order to meet it, then-Secretary Betty Ireland recalled that she "lived and breathed HAVA."

The implementation timeline, giving states roughly three years to build and activate the registration database, posed particular difficulties in states with part-time legislatures. In North Dakota, the legislature only meets once every two years for no more than eighty days. Secretary Jaeger recalled that HAVA was enacted in October 2002, with an implementation deadline of December 31, 2005. With the North Dakota legislature scheduled to meet for the first months of 2003, with a subsequent hiatus until January 2005, Jaeger had "only weeks to prepare a package for the legislature that met in January. I could not wait from 2003 to 2005 to put the legislation in place. We had to be on top of it immediately."

The legislation also posed a challenge for the Secretaries who had been elected in 2002, a few days after HAVA was signed into law, as they also had to act quickly to grapple fully with all of the changes the Act brought to their office. One was Arkansas Secretary Charlie Daniels, who took office in January 2003 and whose first day on the job was spent "trying to figure out what HAVA meant. And that was a big challenge." Daniels met with some of the authors of the legislation to get a sense of the Congressional intent that underlay the reforms. In January 2005, Election Systems & Software (ES&S) was awarded a $5 million contract to implement Arkansas's new voter registration system, NOVA (the Network of Voters in Arkansas). NOVA became fully operational as a centralized voter registration database in January 2006, enabling Arkansas's county election officials to share information with each other, the Division of Motor Vehicles, the Department of Health, and the Arkansas Department of Community Correction in an effort to maintain accurate election rolls.

While some states had existing statewide databases prior to HAVA's passage, the vast majority of states left the management of voter registration to local jurisdictions. As a result, the bulk of the work many Secretaries experienced was

15 Help America Vote Act of 2002, Pub. L. No. 107-252, 1666 Stat. 116 (codified in scattered sections of 42 U.S.C.).

laboring to collect and collate the various registration lists. In Maine, Secretary Dunlap gathered approximately one million voter registration records from more than 503 municipalities, each with separate voter lists into a single system. The records were previously maintained in a variety of ways on the local level, often times on paper or cards, or an assortment of computer programs, and sometimes stored in the home of the municipal voter registrar. Dunlap recalled that "some of the lists were quite sophisticated and some were literally, not written down."

Indiana Secretary Todd Rokita threw "all of the county systems into the river" and built a $23 million database that could be updated in real time. To Rokita, the key was to get "buy-in at the local level." He took the time to "build grassroots support [for the centralized database] at the county level" for the development of the database. Rokita also hired an additional staff member to manage the project, which enabled the rest of his staff to concentrate on other projects. In Idaho, Secretary Ben Ysursa also hired an additional staff person to devote their time to HAVA and implementation, and Pennsylvania Secretary Pedro Cortés similarly worked to unite the various counties in his state "to go from 60 individual databases to one statewide database."

Kansas Secretary Thornburgh took one of the most creative approaches, naming the new database "ELVIS," short for "ELection Voter Information System." ELVIS went "live" statewide on December 29, 2005, just two days short of the federal deadline. Thornburgh also worked to create a partnership between the Secretary of State's office and a number of other Kansas state agencies, including the Department of Corrections, Division of Motor Vehicles, and the Office of Vital Statistics, to ensure the database would be updated to remove ineligible voters. The careful development of ELVIS was crucial to Thornburgh, who views "the database of voter registration [as] the cornerstone around which all elections are conducted" and the "heartbeat that everything else operates from." In an effort to be sensitive to the concerns of local elections officials, who heretofore had maintained full responsibility for the registration lists, Thornburgh

> "went to the counties and said look, you tell me what you want. You tell me what it's supposed to look like, taste like, smell like, and we'll build it. And I made sure that everybody was at the table, even those who disagreed with me. And those who disagreed with me, I demanded that they stay at the table with us. And I told the counties, under federal law, I have to own the database. However, you own the data. I will never touch a line of data, you're the one who decides who gets entered, stays on, stays off, whatever the case may be."

And in Oregon, then-Secretary Bill Bradbury was working to implement the state's vote-by-mail system when the HAVA mandate came down. Vote-by-mail, enacted via a ballot initiative in 1998, meant that all ballots in Oregon would be cast through the mail instead of at a polling place. HAVA's mandate for a statewide registration database came quickly on the heels of the initial transition to vote-by-mail elections, and Bradbury was required to oversee the combined transition. But to Bradbury, moving to a statewide voter registration system helped ensure that the final shift to vote-by-mail occurred smoothly. Because under the pre-HAVA system, "a voter would move from the city of Portland to the city of Eugene, which are two cities in Oregon about 110 miles apart. They would be registered in both places. So, a lot of ballots would have to be mailed, and then the person has moved, so the ballots either be returned [and the postage wasted], or there might be instances where someone could get two ballots in the mail," one sent to their old address and one to their new address. And, Bradbury noted, "when you have vote-by-mail, you are not voting in person so it is easier to cast more than one ballot."

But the HAVA statewide registration system eliminated that potential for fraud. Now in Oregon "every voter is only registered once." The Secretary of State "sends out ballots to the address listed on your voter registration forms, and if the post office returns the ballot and says us that you've moved, you're then moved from an active voter to an inactive voter and you won't be mailed another ballot until you have contacted the elections office." And as a result of the transition, Bradbury believes Oregon is "going to have the cleanest voter roll in this country in about a year or two, because … you're moved to inactive status as soon as the post office returns the ballot and says that you do not live there anymore."

Implementation of HAVA: Upgrading Voting Technology

The second pivotal aspect to HAVA was the billions of dollars it allocated for states to update their voting technology, particularly to accommodate voters with disabilities. To Secretary Ireland, the funds to upgrade the voting machines were "the greatest thing HAVA did for West Virginia, because we now have accessible machines for those folks who are disabled. And that is a wonderful thing for a blind person for the first time to be able to vote." Idaho Secretary of State Ben Ysursa, for example, entered into a $6 million contract with Election Systems and Software (ES&S) to purchase 932 AutoMARK voting devices in order to meet the HAVA requirement to provide at least one accessible voting device in each polling place by 2006. As a result, Ysursa commented at the time, "many people with disabilities, particularly visually impaired voters, would now be able to experience the same privacy and independence the other voters take for granted."

In Nebraska, Secretary John Gale stated that "for probably the last 30 years, 45 counties were still hand counting ballots, and they didn't have the capability to spend the money to overcome that handicap." As a result, Nebraska

> "had this enormous disparity between the 30 larger counties that had modern equipment and the some 60 that did not. So with HAVA we had the opportunity to ensure that every county had optical scan equipment and that has been, been a tremendous benefit and blessing to the smaller counties because they are not up until 2 or 3 o'clock a.m. hand counting ballots."

Without HAVA, Gale believes, "I don't think the state would ever have probably come up with the money" to upgrade their voting technology

> "because there was kind of an entrenched attitude in Nebraska that elections are county based and county financed and the states should not be stepping in and providing that funding. With that kind of traditional notion, I doubt the state would have ever done what HAVA did, which was in effect to provide Nebraska with $22 million dollars … [to enable] … this top down purchase of equipment for the whole state so that we have a uniform system of Automark for the handicap and visually impaired, and we also have optical scan equipment."

Markowitz agreed with Gale's remarks, reflecting that "HAVA for the first time, put money, federal money in the hands of localities to buy equipment." But the unfortunate price to many states, she noted, was that the cart was put before the horse. "People were given money [and] were hired to spend it" before the federal government had

> "set standards for the equipment that's being purchased. And so everybody, rightly, bought the state of the art equipment. And the only best state of the art equipment on the market were touch screen [electronic] machines, of course none of which had paper trails, because that wasn't seen as desirable or the standard when these initial purchases were being made."

Then the 2004 election occurred. Allegations swirled questioning whether electronic voting machines could be "hacked." Many questioned the overall security of a technology where a voter could enter their choice and walk away without any paper record to later verify that the machine had accurately recorded their choice.[16]

Out of this increased concern over the security of the electronic machines came a call for some sort of "voter verified paper trail," enabling voters to verify that their vote was accurately cast and counted. To Secretary Bysiewicz in Connecticut, HAVA was

> "a great thing in that we bought our voting machines, but I don't think it really achieved its goal because I think 40% of the voting machines in our country have no paper trail. So tell me what HAVA accomplished if we have no paper trail in half of the states in the country. I'm very pleased to have the money, but show me the paper trail because I know we're secure in Connecticut but I'm not so sure about other places."

16 See Chapter 8 for more details of these allegations and their ramifications.

Some states had already invested millions of dollars in equipment that did not provide for such a paper trail, only to see their state legislatures subsequently respond to the public outcry for greater security with legislation to require a paper trail. Those states, Markowitz noted, were "stuck with new state laws that would require them to ditch those machines or to add on a paper trail, which may make it more difficult to run the election, because whenever you do an equipment overlay there is a much higher failure rate in the equipment."

Secretary Ireland waited for the legislature to act "to see what they were going to do regarding mandating a paper trail." The West Virginia legislature did just that in April of 2005, and Ireland subsequently reviewed and vetted proposals from potential vendors and purchased machines by the December 31, 2005 deadline. And Secretary Charlie Daniels in Arkansas, began working to implement HAVA immediately after being sworn into office in January 2003. Daniels set up a bipartisan committee comprised of local election officials, disability groups, members of political parties, public members, partnering state agencies, and minority groups. The committee collectively felt electronic voting machines, or "DREs," were the best option—one county had already had such a machine. Daniels recalls that many of the local elections officials "chose the DREs because they didn't need paper ballots" and at that time there were minimal concerns about paper trails. But then just before the equipment was purchased, a freshman state legislator began "pushing for a voter verification system with a paper trail."

Like Gale in Nebraska and a handful of other Secretaries, South Dakota Secretary Chris Nelson avoided the chaos around paper trails and electronic voting by purchasing optical scan machines, which electronically scan and count paper ballots, coupled with an AutoMARK touch screen machine for voters with limited sight or otherwise in need of additional assistance. Nelson says he "chuckle[s] in hindsight because a lot of the states that were going off on the DRE track now are swinging around and going to what I call the South Dakota model, where they are using the optical scan and the AutoMarks."

Implementation of HAVA: The Election Assistance Commission

HAVA also created a new federal agency, the Election Assistance Commission, to "serve as a national clearinghouse and resource for the compilation of information and review of procedures with respect to the administration of Federal elections."[17] The four member bipartisan commission, appointed by the President with the advice and consent of the Senate, is also charged with developing standards of compliance with HAVA requirements and auditing the use of federal funding distributed under the legislation.

17 Help America Vote Act of 2002, Pub. L. No. 107-252, 1666 Stat. 116 (codified in scattered sections of 42 U.S.C.).

The EAC has maintained a somewhat rocky but improving relationship with the Secretaries. In February 2005, New Hampshire Secretary Bill Gardner spearheaded a resolution that passed at a NASS convention, which asked Congress not to reauthorize the EAC. Gardner argued about the risk that "five years from now, all of a sudden we find out that they take over the whole elections process at the federal level." A few days after the resolution was passed, the four members of the commission came to speak to the Secretaries, who were still convened at the NASS conference "about keeping the eye on the prize," Gardner recalled. But to Gardner and other Secretaries, the functions of the EAC threatened state sovereignty. "This isn't a personal issue," Gardner said, "this is an issue of whether the states ought to be able to run their elections like they have been throughout the history of our country."

Conclusion

The brouhaha over the EAC specifically and HAVA more generally is reflective of concerns that many Secretaries have over Congress micromanaging election administration. Their unease rests primarily on what they see as Congress's effort to develop a "one size fits all" approach to what state officials see as a diverse process. South Dakota Secretary Chris Nelson questioned how much longer Congress would continue "trying to monkey with state election procedures." Idaho Secretary Ben Ysursa jokingly referred to HAVA as the "Help Florida Vote Act," noting that despite his appreciation of the funding it provided to his state, "HAVA to us again was another one size fits all" solution. Ysursa admits that HAVA "certainly was needed in some states, and it has been helpful" in Idaho, but maintains the bill was primarily "an insidious federal intrusion into our area of elections." He felt that "the folks on the Potomac have no idea what goes on out here [in Idaho] and how elections are run. I mean we still have 14 counties in Idaho that run on paper ballots. They are not going to change. I am not going to tell them to change. It's local preference." North Dakota Secretary Al Jaeger echoed Ysursa's concern, noting also his belief that "in some cases we could have made better use of taxpayer money. Because even if it comes from the federal government, it still comes from the taxpayers."

Beyond their concerns about micromanagement, several Secretaries also expressed concern that compliance with federal mandates took up so much of their time that they were unable to explore other reforms or improvements to elections in their states that may have been necessary. Maine Secretary Matt Dunlap specifically expressed that HAVA compliance "has really absorbed most of our attention over the last few years." South Dakota Secretary Nelson noted that he's spent the bulk of his tenure as Secretary "just following what Congress has tried to do, and reacting to what they are trying to do. Most of which I think is not good, not healthy" because it takes away from the ability of states to serve as incubators of innovation.

But Nelson also emphasized a silver lining, noting that Congress in recent years appears to be listening more to the voices of Secretaries on the ground. He pointed specifically to a "success" of the Secretaries of keeping legislation proposed by U.S. Congressman Rush Holt from being passed. Holt's bill, the "Voter Confidence and Increased Accessibility Act," specifically would have mandated that every voting system allow for audits and a paper trail. As Congress debated the legislation, Nelson saw that many representatives "learned a lot from the HAVA experience," and are now "coming to elections people and saying 'how can we work with you,' as opposed to a 'shove this down your throat' concept."

And Kansas Secretary Ron Thornburgh, after his time on Capitol Hill seeking to work with congressional leaders and offer the perspective of a statewide election official, similarly expressed caution, mixed with optimism, that Congress and Secretaries of State can work collectively and collaboratively to further their mutual goals of advancing access and integrity in the electoral system. Thornburgh admits to witnessing "a tremendous growth in the federal government's willingness to federalize local and state processes. And not understanding the states' rights, or unwilling to recognize the states' rights argument. And the fact that we don't have a federal election in the United States of America, we have fifty state elections." But in his view, it is the responsibility of Secretaries and voters to work to communicate that "simple concept" to federal lawmakers.

With further collaboration in both directions, it becomes possible to develop systems that allow for local flexibility, leadership, and discretion, while also creating guidelines, standards, parameters, and support on the federal level. To Thornburgh, state and local election officials "need support and they need guidelines. They need parameters to work with. But then they've got to have the ownership and the flexibility." And at the end of the day, if state and local officials feel like they can maintain some ownership over the election administration process, "they are going to be much more likely to engage and do it properly."

Kansas Secretary of State
Ron Thornburgh

First Elected: 1994

To Ron Thornburgh, "The job of elections is very simple: to make sure that every vote that deserves to be counted is counted, and that every citizen who has the right, has the opportunity to vote." And the job of Secretary of State was one that came naturally to him since he "kind of grew up in the office." Thornburgh began working for the Kansas Secretary of State as a college sophomore, when he worked in the mail room as the Secretary's driver. After college, he "went to work in the office and worked my way up through the ranks. And I ultimately ran [for the position as Secretary] and won."

Thornburgh's intimate knowledge of the workings of the office helped him transition quickly to the position, because "there weren't a lot of unexpected elements to the job itself." But what he did not expect was the increased role of the federal government in the elections process in the years following the 2000 presidential election. Thornburgh was the incoming president of NASS in the year immediately following that fateful election. At the time, he recalled, "Congress was highly prepared to overreact. And they were ready to move election responsibility from the county courthouse to Congress. They wanted to move everything to Washington."

But as Thornburgh has sought to stress throughout his career as Kansas Secretary of State, "The rationale behind federal intervention has to be to provide support and resources and in some cases, guidance." At the same time, "We have to be very careful because one size rarely fits anybody. And we need systems that allow for flexibility and leadership at the local and state level." Running elections, to Thornburgh "really is rocket science in that you have to get it right the first time. You're not allowed do-overs."

Chapter 4
The Secretary as Voter Advocate

> "I view my role as the chief advocate for voters. I take the side of the voter from the very beginning of the process, which is registrations, all the way through to ensuring that the equipment is appropriate and that the tallies are correct and that we audit."
>
> California Secretary of State Debra Bowen

The state's chief elections official has an unparalleled role as the primary advocate for voters' rights in their state. Like no other government official at the state or national level, Secretaries have an unmatched and critical bully pulpit from which to push for the implementation of policies and laws that reflect the needs of the voters in their state. It is uniquely within their purview to evaluate concerns that their citizens experience in voting and to work to ensure that improvements are made where necessary to promote an accessible and accurate democracy.

Like California Secretary Debra Bowen, many recent and current Secretaries take this role very seriously and see it as their principal duty. Across the country there are scores of examples of Secretaries working together or independently to advocate for reforms seeking to improve the voter's experience and, in the words of Missouri Secretary of State Robin Carnahan, "Make it easier to vote and harder to cheat."

In the years following the 2000 Presidential election, many Secretaries acted in a variety of ways to advocate for voters on a statewide level. Nevada Secretary Ross Miller formed an election integrity task force, in conjunction with the Attorney General, the U.S. Attorney Generals, and the FBI, to respond to any claims of fraud or intimidation at the polling place that could affect voters' confidence in the electoral process. Secretary Betty Ireland in West Virginia created a Voter Hall of Fame to celebrate and recognize registered voters who have voted for over fifty consecutive years. The creation of the hall of fame elicited "wonderful stories about election days in the past from dedicated voters," Secretary Ireland noted. And recently in Mississippi, Secretary of State Delbert Hosemann worked—unsuccessfully—to promote legislation to re-enfranchise ex-offenders who lose their voting rights under state law. With the exception of those convicted of rape and murder, Hosemann's proposal would have allowed convicted felons to have their voting rights restored two years after serving their sentence, including probation.

The Secretary and Collaborations with Voters

To Vermont Secretary Deb Markowitz, the source of true voter advocacy on the statewide level comes from being proactive and creative in addressing voters' concerns. After every election cycle, Markowitz reviews which communities and constituencies throughout her state have low levels of voter participation. Her office then works with organizations that focus specifically on voter turnout for those populations or generally in order to "look at ways that we can begin to reach those non-voting populations." Markowitz recalled that when she first became Secretary, her review of low turnout populations revealed that the lowest levels of participation were among people who couldn't get to their polling places, because "either they were working, they didn't have good transportation, or they lived in really rural areas."

One of Markowitz's first major initiatives was promoting no-reason absentee ballots for those populations, using public service announcements, radio advertising, and brochures that said on the cover, "Vote early, vote-by-mail, just vote." Markowitz partnered with some major businesses and industries to pass brochures out to their workers, and with the Vermont women's commission and other groups to distribute the brochures. Markowitz consistently emphasized that any voter, for no reason, "could ask for a ballot to be mailed to them, or you could pick one up, or could just go to the clerks' office and vote right then. And that anybody could do it; you didn't need to provide any reason at all." As a result of that educational campaign, early absentee ballot use jumped from 4 percent to 20 percent of the total votes cast.

Secretaries Robin Carnahan in Missouri and Jennifer Brunner in Ohio engaged in a similar proactive study of problems voters experienced in elections in their states. Following the 2006 election, Secretary Carnahan conducted a post-election assessment that found, in some places, two- to three-hour wait times for people seeking to cast their ballot. It was a problem that in her view was "unacceptable" and could be cured through allowing for early voting, adequate numbers of ballots, and better training of poll workers.

Carnahan placed those three reforms at the top of her agenda for improvements to implement prior to the November 2008 election.[1] Her view was that voters' "confidence in the elections, and in the results of the elections, often comes from the personal experience they have in a polling place on election day." She noted that the experience is affected by everything from "how the polling place is set up, [to] how long they have to stand in line, [to] how well the people who are running that polling place [are] doing." Thus upon taking office, Carnahan advanced her role as a voter advocate with a focus on both the "mechanical" aspect of running elections, "whether that be ensuring that all these counties and polling places have enough ballots so that people aren't having to stand in line and wait for

1 For a copy of Carnahan's full report, see: www.sos.mo.gov/elections/votersfirst (accessed Nov. 1, 2009).

more ballots, or machines," and the more "personal" aspect to elections, "which is making sure the poll workers are well trained and provide the kind of expertise and leadership in the polling place to make sure it goes well."

When Ohio Secretary Jennifer Brunner was elected in 2006, she created the Ohio Voting Rights Institute to develop methods of improving the accessibility of Ohio elections. The Ohio VRI has developed a "Grads Vote," a program to provide voter registration forms to every graduating high school senior, has secured private foundation funding to work with the U.S. Postal Service to include voter registration forms in government moving packets, and has partnered with the Overseas Vote Foundation to make voting access easier through online absentee ballot applications for overseas and military voters.

Following the 2008 election, Brunner also convened a daylong session to review the problems that emerged in the Ohio election cycle. The purpose of the "Ohio Elections Summit," held on December 2, 2008, was to review the November 4, 2008 election and to create a report with recommendations to improve Ohio's elections process.[2] The report's senior authors were Lawrence Norden, senior counsel for the nonpartisan nonprofit Brennan Center and Jessie Levin, an attorney with another nonprofit organization called the Advancement Project. Also involved in the Summit and report were some of the country's leading election administration scholars and voter advocates. Brunner's goal was for the Summit's report to assist her office in "us[ing] this election as a springboard to solidify best election practices that guarantee the strongest protections of democracy for the highest voter confidence."[3]

In Pennsylvania, Secretary Pedro Cortés regularly convenes an election reform group comprised of individuals representing various communities that have "traditionally not exercised the franchise at the same proportional level as the majority population." The group meets quarterly and advises Secretary Cortés on ways in which he can ensure voting access for all Pennsylvania citizens. Cortés also works with groups like the Pennsylvania Independent Living Council—attending their conferences, meeting with their board, etc.—to ensure he is able to be an informed advocate for ensuring that voters with disabilities enjoy equal access to the polls. Similarly, in Connecticut, Secretary Bysiewicz's office has worked closely with a number of groups, such as the League of Women Voters and Common Cause, and seeks to use her office "as a statewide platform for needed reform."

Other Secretaries view their role as voter advocate includes blocking changes to the law that would impede voting. Former Secretary Bill Bradbury in Oregon, for example, observed in his state a "small group of citizens in Oregon that believe

---

2 Lawrence Norden, *Final Report 2008–2009 Ohio Election Summit and Conference*, April 2009, available at: http://brennan.3cdn.net/9ccb57cb5de1711173_nkm6bqc3y.pdf.

3 *Brunner Announces Bipartisan Summit to Study Election, Voting Process*, Columbus Dispatch, Nov. 7, 2008, http://www.columbusdispatch.com/live/content/local_news/stories/2008/11/07/election_summit.html?sid=101.

that our voter rolls are completely overrun with non-citizens who are registering to vote." This group is "convinced that we should require [all voters to present] a passport or a birth certificate" in order to vote. That reform, Bradbury said, "will happen over my dead body, because that disenfranchises a *huge* number of legitimate Oregon residents and U.S. citizens" who don't have access to those documents. In addition, Bradbury noted, in his view the proposal is "trying to solve a problem that doesn't really exist" and he's used his position as Secretary to stop "those kinds of reforms" that in his view would do more harm than good to Oregon voters.

The Secretary and Voter Registration

Beyond these various programs and perspectives, a concrete area where a state's chief election administrator embodies the role of chief voter advocate is in their management of voter registration. California Secretary Debra Bowen took this issue head on when she became Secretary in 2006, instituting a top to bottom review of the voter registration process. Finding the state's voter registration form "complicated and hard to use," Bowen redesigned it. She concluded that "if you want people to register and you put a form in front of them that looks like a tax form you're going to dissuade some people from registering, or you'll have errors." So she "literally just went through from a usability standpoint how complicated is the language, are the instructions easy to understand. The form had all of the instructions down at the bottom in a little footnote." After Bowen, who sees herself as "the analyst for voters, the advocate, always on the lookout for making sure that the people's wishes are expressed and counted at the polls," finished redesigning the voter registration card, the card went "from 1,250 words to 700." And, Bowen notes, "We were able to remove a lot of excess verbiage to make the form more intuitive and to eliminate some of the voters' confusion."

The requirements for voter registration are generally established through state law, with the exception of the federal Help America Vote Act (HAVA), National Voter Registration Act (NVRA), and Voting Rights Act (VRA).[4] Most significantly, the Help America Vote Act of 2002 mandated the creation of a statewide voter database, which in most states meant placing control of the voter registration data in the hands of the Secretary of State. Upon that delegation of authority, Secretaries immediately took center stage in overseeing the voter registration process.

The NVRA requires states to allow individuals to register to vote when they apply for a driver's license, and also mandates that states provide and accept voter registration forms at several state agencies.[5] The law also requires that states accept a national voter registration form. In addition, Section 202 of the VRA permits otherwise qualified residents of a state to vote in any presidential

4 42 U.S.C. 1973gg (2006).

5 *Id.*

election, regardless of any state residency requirement, so long as the individual registers to vote prior to thirty days before the election.[6] The Act also allows voters who move to another state less than thirty days before a presidential election to vote in their former state.[7]

Every state but North Dakota requires that citizens register to vote, and eight states—Iowa, Minnesota, Wisconsin, Maine, Idaho, Montana, New Hampshire, Wyoming—allow voters to register on Election Day.[8] Twenty-nine of the remaining forty-one states require voters to register roughly one month prior to Election Day, and twelve others have deadlines ranging from two or three weeks (Oregon, West Virginia, Maryland, New Jersey, Massachusetts, Nebraska, California, Connecticut, Kansas, South Dakota, Alabama) to one week (Vermont).[9]

Historians suggest that registration requirements were originally enacted in the late nineteenth century, post reconstruction for purposes of suppressing the vote of members of certain political parties or racial groups.[10] But the modern justification behind registration laws in these forty-one states is that they promote accuracy and integrity in the electoral process.[11] They prevent voters from voting more than once in multiple locations, for example, or, because they require an administrator to review a registrant's eligibility prior to processing their form, they prevent ineligible individuals from casting a ballot.

That said, stringent registration requirements—particularly when they come far in advance of an election—have been shown to limit access or otherwise harm voter participation rates.[12] The eight states with Election Day registration, for example, have consistently boasted turnout rates several percentage points

---

6 *Id.*

7 *Id.*

8 See, e.g., Idaho Code Ann. § 34-408A (1997) (election day registration); Minn. Stat. § 201.061 (2004) (registration on or before election day); Wisc. Stat. § 6.29 (2007) (late registration in person).

9 Vermont's voter registration deadline is set at 5:00 pm the Wednesday before Election Day. http://vermont-elections.org/elections1/registertovote.html (accessed June 1, 2009).

10 Alexander Keyssar, *The Right to Vote* 45 (2001).

11 R. Michael Alvarez, *Voter Registration: Past, Present and Future Written Testimony Prepared for the Commission on Federal Election Reform*, Co-Director, Caltech/MIT Voting Technology http://www.vote.caltech.edu/media/documents/wps/vtp_wp30.pdf at 6 (accessed June 1, 2009).

12 Richard L. Hasen, *Beyond the Margin of Litigation: Reforming U.S. Election Administration to Avoid Electoral Meltdown*, 62 Wash & Lee L. Rev. 937, 965 (2005) ("When a person moves from one state to another or even within a state, the voter must re-register, and the person often must comply with different registration rules. Those citizens who do not speak English may have difficulty finding registration information and forms in their language. Registration deadlines mean that by the time many people start paying attention to a campaign, even a presidential campaign, it may be too late to register to vote").

higher than states that impose registration deadlines.[13] As such, actors within each state electoral system must work to ensure a careful balance is struck between the accuracy and integrity benefits of registration requirements and making registration easy enough so as to reduce the potential for access limitations.

To that end, Secretaries of State are able to play a major role in how registration laws are administered. In 2008, several Secretaries found themselves in the middle of a controversy when they learned that the U.S. Veterans Affairs agency issued a policy to ban nonpartisan voter registration drives in federally-funded VA facilities and homeless shelters, even if the drives were from local or state election administrators, including Secretaries of State. When Connecticut Secretary Susan Byseiwicz heard of the news, she worked to draw public attention to the ban with efforts that included a news conference where she registered voters outside of a New Haven VA hospital and articles in various newspapers, including the New York Times. As a result, Byseiwicz recalled that her office "received hundreds of calls and e-mails and letters from citizens who were outraged and offered their help to volunteer in whatever way they could to get the ban reversed."

Notably, Secretaries pushing to have access to the VA facilities recognized the importance of ensuring such drives were set up at a time and place and conducted in a manner which was not disruptive. Secretary Rokita of Indiana noted the importance of balancing the need to protect veteran's right to vote against the recognition that most VA facilities are hospitals where it may not be appropriate to have anyone going "bed to bed" registering voters. But ultimately the ban was lifted not just to ensure access but out of accuracy concerns as well. California Secretary Bowen emphasized the need not only to "work to try to make sure that our veterans are registered" but also to "ensure that when people return from service that we get the correct address so that we don't send a ballot to Afghanistan to someone who's living in Riverside County" California.

Ultimately, to overturn the ban, Bysiewicz and Washington Secretary Sam Reed organized a national bipartisan effort that included nineteen other Secretaries of State. They wrote a letter to then-Veterans Affairs Secretary James Peake, who has issued the directive banning voter registration drives in VA facilities. The letter noted:

> voter registration drives have historically been a critical outreach tool for veterans in facilities to ensure that they get the opportunity to register to vote. Many veterans simply are not able to get out on their own, rendering registration much more difficult. Likewise, the longstanding practice of allowing facility employees to assist veterans in registering to vote has provided valuable assistance to veterans in need.[14]

---

13 See, e.g., Steve Carbo and Regina Eaton, *The Promise and Practice of Election Day Registration*, in America Votes (Ben Griffith, ed.), a publication of the American Bar Association 72–73 (2008).

14 *Bysiewicz and Blumenthal Request U.S. Secretary of Veterans Affairs Grant Elections Officials Access to Veterans Facilities*, Connecticut Secretary of State, Jul. 2,

Secretary Reed particularly emphasized that it was a "sad irony that the federal agency that is supposed to help our nation's veterans all of a sudden isn't very helpful when it comes to allowing them to exercise one of America's basic rights." According to Secretary Reed, "Assisting patients with voter registration would not harm the appearance of neutrality and it would not violate the Hatch Act. Assisting veterans would not interfere with patient medical care." Peake subsequently reversed the policy in September 2008, ensuring that state and local election administrators and nonpartisan groups were able to access VA facilities to assist officials in registering veteran voters who are receiving care in the final registration period prior to the November 2008 election.

Beyond working to address issues regarding access to the act of registration itself, Secretaries across the country have worked to also offset any other access-impeding side effects of registration requirements efforts to promote participation. Arizona, for example, requires new voters to register at least twenty-nine days prior to an election in order to be eligible to vote in that election, but allows online registration for individuals with a driver's license on file with the state.

And in Washington, Secretary Sam Reed championed online voter registration in 2005 to streamline the process of voter registration and remove the need for local elections officials to enter voter registration forms manually. To Reed, it was a reform that he had "wanted to do for a long time." Instituting it required new legislation, and after Reed tried persuading the legislature to enact the reform only to see it go nowhere, he worked with "student lobbyists for our colleges and universities all fired up and they made it a top priority." Secretary Ross Miller in Nevada attempted to implement online voter registration under existing legislation allowing Nevada registrars to "use a computer to register voters," and South Dakota Secretary Chris Nelson and California Secretary Debra Bowen have both worked to lead the way for the same reform in their state.

A Secretary's actions, however, can also move in the opposite direction, enforcing or administering registration requirements in a way that minimizes participation and creates barriers to the vote. Sometimes these efforts go so far that a court has to intervene to enforce federal law or protect the constitutional right to vote, but not before any damage is done. For example, nonprofit organizations registered under 501(c)3 of the tax code are permitted under federal law to conduct voter registration drives. In fact, many citizens register to vote through the drives of one of several nonprofit organizations, making their role in the registration process significant in ensuring access and promoting participation. On June 14, 2004, a nonprofit organization in Georgia submitted several voter registration applications of individuals seeking to vote in a primary election on July 20, 2004.[15] Three days later, Georgia's then-Secretary of State Cathy Cox rejected all of the registrations,

---

2008, available at: http://www.sots.ct.gov/sots/lib/sots/releases/2008/7.2.08_bysiewicz_blumenthal_send_letter.pdf.

15 *Charles H. Wesley Educ. Found., Inc. v. Cox*, 324 F. Supp. 2d 1358 (N.D. Ga. 2004).

because they were delivered to her office in a bundle and were not collected in the presence of an authorized individual, both of which violated her regulation broadly interpreting the Georgia election code.[16]

The nonprofit organizations sued in federal court in order to have their registrations accepted. On July 1, 2004, less than three weeks prior to Election Day, the court ruled that Secretary Cox's actions violated the National Voter Registration Act, and ordered her to process the applications and enjoined her office from rejecting any additional voter registration applications on similar grounds.[17] Though litigation resolved the issue, at least two weeks in June were lost during which nonprofit organizations could have collected and submitted additional registrations, but were unable to do so until a federal court issued an injunction against the Secretary's policy. The policy was later formally nullified in a consent decree between the Secretary and the nonprofit organizations.[18]

In response to the court's decision, the Georgia Election Board, on which the Georgia Secretary of State wields considerable influence, amended their registration regulations to instead prohibit any nonprofit organizations from collecting and submitting voter registration applications unless they were "sealed" and also

---

16 Court's explanation: "Georgia law permits voter registration by mail. O.C.G.A. § 21-2-223. That section of the Georgia code provides as follows: 'The Secretary of State shall design, publish, and distribute voter registration application forms with which a person may apply to register to vote by completing and mailing the form to the Secretary of State.' O.C.G.A. § 21-2-223(a). The Secretary of State interprets that section of Georgia law to mean that 'a person' may register by sending one application in an individual envelope to the Secretary of State. The state contends that sending in a bundle of applications in one envelope is not permitted under § 21-2-223. … In the letter the Secretary of State's office sent informing plaintiffs' counsel that it was rejecting the bundled applications, it indicated that it could not accept the package because 'the Georgia Election Code does not allow for the acceptance or collection of voter registration applications by any person other than a registrar, a deputy registrar, or a person authorized to accept voter registration applications.' The Georgia Code places restrictions on 'additional registration places' (which include voter registration drives) in that they may operate only during fixed hours and only if they have been advertised in the local media. O.C.G.A. § 21-2-215. The Rules and Regulations interpreting the Election Code specifically provide that a deputy registrar must be present at any 'additional voter registration place.' Ga. Comp. R. & Regs. r. 183-1-6-.03(3)(k)(1). … The state asserts that it is unable to accept bundled applications precisely because they were collected by someone other than a deputy registrar. So, although the anti-bundling policy is allegedly supported by the provision of Georgia law permitting registration by mail only when the application is mailed by the registrant, it is also a result of the state's insistence that applications be collected by only a registrar or deputy registrar." *Id.* at 1366.

17 *Id.*

18 Edward Still, *Georgia: State Signs Consent Decree on NVRA Compliance*, VoteLaw.com, http://www.votelaw.com/blog/archives/003865.html (accessed Aug. 22, 2009).

forbid the organization to copy completed voter registration applications.[19] In August 2006, the same nonprofit organizations filed another challenge in federal court.[20] Two months later (and one month before the election), the federal district court issued a preliminary injunction barring the enforcement of the regulations, on the grounds that they violated the plaintiffs' first amendment rights to register voters.[21]

In both 2004 and 2006, Secretaries of State in Ohio and Florida also issued regulations that created hurdles for groups seeking to register voters.[22] Like the actions of Georgia's Secretary Cox, these hurdles similarly were the result of an administrator placing integrity concerns high above concerns of access and participation in interpreting state registration requirements, instead of developing efforts to advance both legitimate goals.

In the year leading up to the 2004 presidential election, then-Ohio Secretary Blackwell issued three directives regarding the rejection of voter registration applications.[23] Two of the directives required the rejection of completed voter registration forms that left blank information on citizenship or age, or where the applicant failed to provide driver's license numbers or the last four digits of their Social Security number. The policies were in place for several months before Blackwell, at the behest of the Election Assistance Commission, issued clarifying directives overturning his policy requiring information on citizenship or age.[24] But after a federal court challenge failed based on the Judge's finding that it had been filed too late, Blackwell left in place the requirement that hand-delivered registration forms be rejected if they did not include a driver's license or Social Security number.[25] A third directive, issued in September 2004, just two months before Election Day, required the submission of all voter registration forms be

19 The Regulations provided specifically "No person may accept a completed registration application from an applicant unless such application has been sealed by the applicant. No copies of completed registration applications shall be made. This paragraph shall not apply to registrars and deputy registrars." Ga. Comp. R. & Regs. r. 183-1-6-.03 (3)(o)(2).

20 *Ass'n of Cmty. Orgs. for Reform Now v. Cox*, 2006 U.S. Dist. LEXIS 87080 (D. Ga. 2006).

21 *Id.* at 15–18.

22 Richard Wolf, *New Voter Registration Laws Leave Thousands off the Rolls*, USA Today, Oct. 10, 2006, http://www.usatoday.com/news/washington/2006-10-10-voter-registration-laws_x.htm (describing actions by Secretaries of State in Florida and Ohio that made it difficult for voter registration groups to register voters); see also *Dias v. Hood* (SD Fla. 2004) and *Lucas County Democratic Party et al v. Blackwell* (ND Ohio 2004).

23 For a detailed description of the events surrounding all three directives, see Daniel P. Tokaji, *Early Returns on Election Reform: Discretion, Disenfranchisement, and The Help America Vote Act*, 73 Geo. Wash. L. Rev. 1206, 1224–28 (2004).

24 *Id.* at. 1228.

25 *Id.* at. 1224.

on heavy-stock card paper.[26] As a result, voters—and the nonprofit organizations seeking to register them en masse—were unable to use photo copied forms unless they were reproduced on heavier, and pricier, paper.[27] One month later, after advocates and their attorneys raised the specter of the Voting Rights Act, arguing the potentially discriminatory effect and animus behind the paperweight directive, Blackwell backtracked and withdrew the requirement.[28]

Apart from these examples of Secretaries increasing the severity of already stringent registration requirements, Secretaries of State can also play a pivotal role in ensuring that less stringent registration requirements, such as Election Day registration, are administered in a way that emphasizes and promotes the need for accuracy and integrity. A statewide computer file of all voters that poll workers at each precinct can access and update in "real time" as a voter registers and casts their vote mitigates the fear of citizens traveling from precinct to precinct on Election Day to register and vote in each location.[29] In Montana, for example, computers are installed in polling locations throughout the state to allow election officials to access the voter registration database and register new voters on Election Day. As a result, this minimal registration requirement does not impede participation but is also administered in a way that protects the accuracy and integrity of the democratic process.[30]

Success in ensuring that registration requirements in elections promote both accuracy and access goals can be directly attributed to the actions of a Secretary of State as an advocate for voters. While some scholars have emphasized the negative

26 *Id.* at 1227 (citing Directive No. 2004-31).

27 See also *id.* at 1227–28 (noting that in addition to the "paper weight" directive, Blackwell also required that "certain federal voter registration forms be accepted even on lighter paper weight").

28 See, e.g., Mary Beth Beazley and Edward B. Foley, *Registration Rules: Special Commentary: Stealing Votes Before Election Day*, in The e-Book on Election Law, Sept. 29, 2004, at http://moritzlaw.osu.edu/electionlaw/ebook/part1/eligibility_rules08.html.

29 A similar version to this example is proposed in a recent report published by the Election Law @Moritz Center at The Ohio State University Moritz College of Law. See *From Registration to Recounts: The Election Ecosystems of Five Midwestern States* at 177 available at: http://moritzlaw.osu.edu/electionlaw/joyce/book.pdf ("One uniformly desirable feature would be the ability to correct and update the [registered voter] database from each precinct on Election Day.") See also *id.* (suggesting that to minimize costs concerns about that proposal, "states still could employ electronic poll books, rather than paper ones, that could share information with each other across precincts about who has voted, even if they did not allow changes to the registration information itself").

30 See also Ben Ysursa and Matt Dunlap, *Never Too Late to Vote*, New York Times, May 11, 2007, available at: http://www.nytimes.com/2007/05/11/opinion/11dunlap.html?_r=2&oref=slogin&oref=slogin ("With simple, fair and safe methods to verify voters, and by relying on effective poll-worker training and sophisticated election administration, our states have ensured the integrity of the process while allowing every eligible citizen to cast a ballot").

aspects of this role, arguing for federalized registration as a remedy,[31] if Secretaries of State work consistently and energetically to balance accuracy and access issues as they relate to registration requirements, the holders of this office could be the most appropriate and fitting officials charged with this responsibility.

Secretaries and Voting Access: Increasing the Opportunities to Cast a Ballot

In addition to working to ease restrictions on voter registration while ensuring that the integrity of the registration process is preserved, several Secretaries have embodied the role of voter advocate through efforts to widen the avenues and options for casting a ballot.

In 2008, Ohio Secretary Jennifer Brunner interpreted Ohio election law to allow for a one week window in which voters could both register and cast a ballot at the same time. Under Ohio law, absentee voting is permitted up to thirty-five days before the election, and voter registration closed thirty days before the election, thus creating an overlap of five days in which voters could both register and cast an absentee ballot at any local clerk's office.

And in Missouri, Secretary Robin Carnahan has continuously advocated for the legislature to allow for early voting up to two weeks prior to the election date. In 2005, Carnahan proposed a plan called "Advance Missouri." The plan sought to allow Missouri voters to vote in person up to six weeks prior to the election at a central voting location, and up to two weeks before the election at satellite voting stations throughout the state.

Carnahan admitted her frustration that the reform became mired in partisan politics, emphasizing that the previous Secretary of State, a Republican, backed the same reform. She described the stymied legislation as her "biggest disappointment" and "a great frustration," explaining:

> "the proposal that I've put forward was identical to what my Republican predecessor put forward. When he proposed it, the Republicans were for it and the Democrats were against it; when I proposed it, the Democrats were for it and the Republicans were against it. It's the same proposal without a comma changed. So the frustration to me is that many times, people think there's a political motivation to wanting to change things that have to do with elections. But I think when you're in the elections business, it's not about Democrats or Republicans, it's about democracy and it's about making things easier for voters."

In Idaho, Secretary Ben Ysursa reflected on his work to promote "changes in election law that have improved accessibility for everyone. Many years ago we were advocating no excuse absentee voting. We implemented Election Day

31 Hasen, *Beyond the Margin of Litigation: Reforming U.S. Election Administration to Avoid Electoral Meltdown*, 62 Wash. & Lee L. Rev. 937 (2005).

registration." In 2008, Ysursa's hopes were to transition to "optional all-mail voting" like Idaho's neighbors, Oregon and Washington. Ysursa takes his role of advocating on behalf of all voters in his state seriously because "Idaho used to be near to the top of voter participation. Back in 1980 we were number two behind [Minnesota] in voting age population turnout. And we'd like to get back there."

Secretary Rokita in Indiana, Secretary Thornburgh in Kansas, and Secretary Gale in Nebraska all have similarly been advocating for improved access to voting with the creation of satellite voter centers. In Indiana, Rokita pushed for "Vote Centers" to allow "Hoosiers to vote the way we live, with confidence, and not bound by the traditional precinct structure." To Rokita, the Centers would enable voters to vote "the way we live," without having to worry "about finding the right precinct." Centers were placed in high-traffic, accessible locations, many along public transit lines. Electronic poll books in each location eliminated the possibility of duplicate voting. The Vote Centers were tremendously successful in the November 2008 election, under a pilot program in three counties. Rokita subsequently advocated for an expansion of the Vote Centers to other counties, but hit a snag in the state legislature due to allegations of irregularities in the Centers that Rokita labeled as "partisan."

Rokita's efforts followed similar reforms in Colorado, Kansas, and Nebraska. In Nebraska, the use of early voting at satellite voting sites allowed voters to vote at centralized locations, such as shopping centers, government buildings, hospitals, or college campuses, in the days prior to Election Day. Gale advocated for this reform "to make voting more convenient and accessible for people," as part of a "broad push to reverse a declining interest in voting and make sure our democracy remains vibrant." The law allowed Gale to establish satellite voting sites up to twenty days before an election.

In advocating for the reform, Gale worked to emphasize its benefits for voters throughout his state. He also worked to underscore the need to implement the program with measures in place to protect against fraud. Gale "got both political parties involved in the discussion, and the election commissioners, and the bill passed with minimal opposition."

Once enacted, Gale implemented satellite voting "in a cautious manner," beginning with the May 2006 statewide primary election "to test the concept and its popularity." He began with a pilot project in Lincoln, Nebraska at public libraries because they were "well distributed and neutral sites, they had good parking, and they were compliant" with the Americans with Disabilities Act. But no sooner did his office begin "getting the plan off the ground then the Democratic Party said, 'Now hold it that's not fair, that's a Republican conspiracy to make voting easier for suburban Republicans, because you're not putting it in a site in the downtown location in the center of the city, close to the university, and close to the inner-city people.'" Gale recalls being caught by surprise "because [Democrats] had approved of the process up to that point." He explained that his office did not choose sites in urban areas because they were without adequate parking and were not compliant with the Americans with Disabilities Act. To Gale, "if it's not ADA compliant, it's not on our list" of places to allow for satellite voting.

The pilot program drew such controversy over where locations would be located that Gale decided to put the program on hold. Gale recalled that "until we can all get along and eliminate some of this partisan bickering we are not probably ever going to have satellite voting." "We haven't tried it again," Gale said, "but we hope to someday have satellite voting" in Nebraska.

Conclusion

The difficulties surrounding Gale's efforts in Nebraska and Carnahan's efforts in Missouri, among others, highlights what is perhaps the most significant stumbling block facing Secretaries seeking to use their office to be advocates for voters: partisan bickering. In Kansas, for example, it was only when Democratic Governor Kathleen Sebelius and Republican Secretary of State Ron Thornburgh worked together in 2006 to craft legislation to allow all counties to have the ability to set up satellite advance voting sites that it became possible. Previous efforts had failed due to disagreements between parties over whether only large counties or all counties could qualify to set up such locations. And Brunner's implementation of the "overlap" period in 2008 elicited mountains of litigation brought by the opposing political party.

The lesson here is that Secretaries from both political parties have consistently demonstrated their work as advocates for voters, seeking to enact reforms and implement election law in a way that promotes access for all voters. And those efforts are least successful, or become most costly, when partisanship drives opposition to the programs. Ultimately, it is the voters who lose when those efforts are halted by partisanship, because perhaps their greatest allies in government are held back from playing their role as voter advocates when party politics gets in the way.

And importantly, the solution comes from both Secretaries and voters. Like Gale, Brunner, Carnahan, and Thornburgh, Secretaries must prioritize their role as advocates for voters over their allegiance to any political partisan influence. And they similarly must stand their ground, as Brunner did in 2008 and Thornburgh in 2006, in deference to the needs of voters in their state over pressures from any political party. Voters, in turn, must seek to ensure that Secretaries are aware of their concerns and voting needs. In doing so, Secretaries are better able to adhere to the voters' desires over any other influences.

In other words, both voters and sitting Secretaries must form a partnership of collaboration and communication. In doing so, voters are able to inform and bolster a Secretary's ability to voice their concerns and advocate on their behalf, and Secretaries can ensure that they are being true to the voter's needs in advocating for reforms or changes to election administration, which in turn should embolden them to withstand any pressure from a political party to behave in a way that neglects their role as the voter's advocate.

Minnesota Secretary of State
Mark Ritchie

First Elected: 2006

Minnesota Secretary of State Mark Ritchie is part of a new breed of Secretaries. His path to the Secretary of State office was far from the traditional method of rising through the political party infrastructure. Instead, his work in the decades leading up to his election focused on two of the major substantive responsibilities of the office he now occupies: elections and agriculture.

Originally from Iowa, he spent twenty years as the founder and president of the Minneapolis-based Institute for Agriculture and Trade Policy, a non-profit organization working with businesses, churches, farm organizations, and other civic groups to foster long-term sustainability for Minnesota's rural communities. Ritchie particularly focused on serving the small-scale family farmers, prevalent throughout the state, but his heart was never far from recognizing the importance of voting. He also created the League of Rural Voters, now run by his brother Neil, a grassroots organization committed to raising awareness around issues that affect rural communities and "working to create change by harnessing the power of the ballot box."

In the months leading up to the 2004 election, he took a leave from the Institute he founded to lead National Voice, a national coalition of community-based organizations from across the country that work together to increase nonpartisan civic engagement and voter participation. National Voice, through their "November 2" media campaign, registered over five million new voters nationwide, making the effort one of the largest nonpartisan voter mobilizations in our nation's history.

The expertise he developed has served him well as Secretary, he developed the "80 in 08" campaign, which led to a record 84 percent registration rate of all eligible voters in his state in November 2008. And his role as a political outsider helped ensure he was able to fairly and judiciously oversee a statewide recount in the 2008 Coleman–Franken Senate race, which captured national headlines.

Chapter 5

The Secretary as Voter Educator

> "Although the United States is a bastion of democracy, American voting rates are low compared with other nations. Teaching Americans how to be educated voters is a critical challenge facing all of us."
>
> Nebraska Secretary of State John Gale

To Alabama Secretary of State Beth Chapman, a personally gratifying aspect of her job involves times when she works late in her office and answers the phone only to hear a voter with questions on the other end of the line. The citizen may think they can't vote or may not understand Alabama's rules for absentee voting; either way Chapman herself enjoys being the person on the other end of the line, eagerly embracing her role of providing information to voters on the mechanics of casting their ballot.

The same holds true for Pennsylvania Secretary Pedro Cortés. In 2006, Cortés launched an innovative and robust voter education campaign called "Ready, Set, Vote." The campaign involved everything from efforts to improve poll worker training to providing answers to some of the most commonly asked questions of voters: Am I registered? Where do I vote? What is my polling place? How do I get there? What are these machines like? How do I come prepared? To Cortés, "the bottom line of our campaign is making sure that when a voter comes to vote, the voter is registered, the voter is familiar with the voting machines, the voter knows where their polling place is and how to get there." The information is provided via the web, at www.PAVotes.com, and via a toll free hotline. Cortés also provides several translations of the information for voters with limited English proficiency.

Across the board, voter education is one of the most important—and rewarding—responsibilities of a state's chief elections official. From increased use of the internet to deliver information to voters, to the development and dissemination of voter education guides, to a complete reconfiguration of civic and poll worker education in their state, Secretaries are uniquely positioned to aggressively work to ensure that all democratic actors—from poll workers to voters—are equipped with the important information they need to perform their roles in the electoral process. Each Secretary's work will typically emphasize one, if not all, of these priorities, as a way of furthering their duty as the state's chief voter educator.

The Secretary as Educator: Voting Mechanics

Nearly every Secretary seeks to ensure that voters in their state know "how" to vote. Many employ innovative techniques to ensure that their message travels throughout their state. Former West Virginia Secretary Betty Ireland sent a welcome kit to any registered voter who files a change of address form with the post office, as a reminder to update their voter registration information. Her kit directed voters to her website, www.WVvotes.com, where they can download a voter registration form to fill out and send to their county clerk. Indiana Secretary Todd Rokita used his position to advocate for the creation of an Indiana Voter's Bill of Rights to explain—in English and in Spanish—the rights and responsibilities of every Indiana voter.

Others partner with nonpartisan organizations such as Rock the Vote or the League of Women Voters to disseminate accurate information to community members. Iowa Secretary Michael Mauro, for example, formed "Rock the Caucus" in 2008, in partnership with Rock the Vote and the Iowa New Voters Project to recruit high school students and their friends to participate in the Iowa Caucuses. The program also implemented a "Rock the Caucus" curriculum to teach new potential caucus attendees about the process and encourage them to bring their friends. Several Secretaries also engage in education campaigns targeting young or new voters. Secretary Bowen in California uses social networking media such as Facebook to reach young voters, while Secretaries Markowitz, Byseiwicz, Thornburgh and others visit high schools and college campuses in their states to register students to vote.

Vermont Secretary Deb Markowitz was one of the first Secretaries to begin to fully utilize the power of the internet to further voter education. In 2002 her office developed a video, posted on her website, designed to lead Vermonters through the voting process. The video, designed to demystify the process of voting, walked the viewer through the entire voting process. The video not only illustrated to first time voters what they could expect at the polls, it also provided answers to common questions about voter's rights and responsibilities, including what to do if one makes a mistake on their ballot.

After his election in 2006, Nevada Secretary Ross Miller's initial focus was to overhaul his website to create a portal of voter information tools and dispel confusion over the mechanics of voting. Miller placed the state's entire file of registered voters online at www.silverstate08.com, where voters are able to verify that they are registered to vote, view their voting history, their elected officials, and their polling location. The evening before the 2008 presidential caucuses in Nevada, over 30,000 people visited the website to find the location of their caucus. A Similar site exists in Michigan, where voters can verify their registration information and voting location at www.michigan.gov/sos.

Changes in the law are a frequent source of voter confusion. In 2004, in the first major federal election following the passage of the Help America Vote Act (HAVA), voters in most states were asked to use new voting machines or new systems of voter registration.

Several Secretaries developed initiatives to ensure their voters were prepared to vote and aware of these changes. In 2008, Kentucky Secretary Trey Grayson traveled to the largest counties in his state to highlight new voting machines. Called eScans, the machines scan voters' selections on printed ballots and integrate vote totals from absentee and electronic voting systems to produce a single set of election reports. In 2006, Kansas Secretary Ron Thornburgh created a "Vote! Kansas" initiative to inform voters of HAVA's identification requirements for first time voters. The program included the development of sample ballots and the posting of a list of voters' rights and responsibilities at every polling place. Thornburgh also created an "ELection Voter Information System." The system, dubbed "ELVIS," included a secure centralized database of all registered voters, in furtherance of the Help America Vote Act requirement of a centralized voter database.

In Montana, former Secretary Bob Brown created a plan with the help of an Election Reform Advisory Committee he formed to help create and implement HAVA.[1] The plan included efforts to develop workshops and educational material for elections officials on all of the new voting equipment and the implementing of the new identification requirements. Brown also reached out to the Montana Historical Society to develop a teaching module on the history of elections that included and explained the HAVA changes for presentations in schools and to civic groups. In 2008, former Montana Secretary Brad Johnson built upon Brown's plans to develop Voter Information Pamphlets that included HAVA information that were mailed to every voting household in Montana before federal general elections. His office also developed grassroots education efforts such as booths at county fairs and outdoors shows to provide voters with the chance to learn about HAVA provisions and Montana's voting systems.

Upon taking office in 2008, Texas Secretary Hope Andreade surveyed all 254 counties, compiled a list of best practices, and developed resources to supplement locally developed voter education materials. Secretary Andreade also appointed a virtual voter education advisory committee composed of voter advocacy groups and other interested stakeholders to advise the Secretary. The committee recommended, developed and disseminated a Project V.O.T.E. (Voters of Tomorrow through Education) Student Mock Election Curriculum for teachers on how to conduct mock elections for Texas students, kindergarten through 12th grade. Over a half million students participated in the 2004 Texas student mock election.[2]

---

1 Montana Secretary of State Bob Brown, *Preliminary State Plan: Help America Vote Act of 2002*, Montana Dept. of State, May 27, 2003, http://sos.mt.gov/Elections/forms/HAVA/HAVA%20State%20Plan.pdf (accessed Aug. 22, 2009).

2 Texas Secretary of State Geoffrey Connor, *Amended Texas State Plan Pursuant to the Help America Vote Act of 2002*, Texas Dept. of State, Jan. 2005, http://www.sos.state.tx.us/elections/forms/stateplan0105.pdf (accessed Aug. 22, 2009).

Aside from HAVA, Secretaries also spread the word to voters about how several changes to state election laws may affect their participation in the election process. For example, the 2008 election cycle was the first where Iowa voters were able both to register to vote and to cast their ballots on the same day. In order to ensure voters in his state were aware of the new provision and all of its requirements, Secretary Mauro created an Election Day Registration instructional video, which he posted on his website. The video trained both precinct officials and voters on what to expect under the new law. In particular, it emphasized the identification requirements that voters seeking to register on Election Day would need to provide and the penalties for submitting false information when registering to vote.

One of the most significant reforms at the state and federal level in recent years has been the enactment of photo identification requirements for voters. In 2002, HAVA created a federal photo identification requirement for all first time voters.

At the behest of a federal court order, Georgia Secretary Karen Handel implemented the most extensive photo ID education campaign in the country. In 1997 the Georgia General Assembly enacted a law that required voters to present identification in order to vote. The law allowed voters to use such identification as birth certificates, social security cards, a copy of a current utility bill, etc. Voters who did not have one of the seventeen forms of ID enumerated in the statute were entitled to vote so long as they signed a statement under oath that he/she was the person identified on the elector's checklist.[3]

In 2005 the Georgia Assembly adopted an additional photo identification requirement for every voter. The new law required that all voters present government-issued photo identification as an absolute condition to being admitted to the polls.[4] The main argument given in support of this legislation was the prevention of voter fraud, despite the fact that former Georgia Secretary Cathy Cox, who was Secretary at the time of the law's enactment, testified that there had been no documented cases of voter fraud by voters misrepresenting their identity in the state of Georgia.

After a preliminary injunction barred the enforcement of the new law in the 2006 election,[5] a federal district court upheld the law,[6] concluding that the ID requirement did not impose a significant burden on registered voters and was rationally related to the state's objective of combating voter fraud. But the court also required Handel to engage in a significant voter education effort in order to minimize any additional burdens the law placed on voters.

---

3 O.C.G. § 21-2-417.

4 The legislature later amended the law in 2006 to the removal of the requirement that a voter take an affidavit of poverty to obtain a voter ID without charge from the Department of Drivers Services. In place of the affidavit of poverty the voter only has to swear "that he or she desires an identification card in order to vote … and that he or she does not have any other form of identification that is acceptable" and to "produce evidence that he or she is registered to vote in Georgia."

5 *Common Cause/Georgia v. Billups*, 439 F. Supp. 2d 1294 (N.D. Ga. 2006).

6 *Common Cause/Georgia v. Billups*, 504 F. Supp. 2d 1333 (N.D. Ga. 2007).

Handel began by sending a written notice of the requirement to all registered Georgia voters who did not have a Georgia driver's license or state identification card.[7] Handel, emphasizing her commitment to fulfilling the court order mandating an extensive voter education effort, explained that she took the imperative to educate voters on the new identification requirements "very seriously." In developing her comprehensive plan, Handel and her staff "really wanted to look at how we could [proactively] reach individual voters who might not have a photo ID." Recognizing a driver's license as the most prevalent form of photo ID, Handel "ran a match between our voter registration list and the drivers' license list. And we came up with a list of people that didn't match, and it was a list that included people who may have had a passport, [or] a military ID" but kept everyone on the list because "we wanted to [contact] the biggest pool of voters, not the smallest pool of voters."

Her comprehensive outreach program included several phases. The first, began in August 2007 and involved the creation of a website, GaPhotoID.com, and a toll-free hotline. Both listed the required forms of photo identification and instructed voters how to obtain a Georgia Voter Identification Card, included a frequently-asked-questions (FAQ) section, and detailed contact information for voters with additional questions. Handel also mailed information to roughly 77,000 voters in counties with upcoming elections. The second phase began in September 2007 with the mailing of an educational pamphlet on how to obtain free photo identification to over 166,000 registered voters in Georgia, who were not listed as having a state driver's license or state identification card in the Georgia Department of Drivers Services records. Handel also placed public service announcements on cable television and advertised on several radio stations, including during broadcasts of Atlanta Falcons' games. She also distributed information to public libraries and other facilities, while conducting mandatory training sessions for all county elections officials and poll workers. A few months later, in January 2008, Handel initiated a third phase, sending reminder letters to 80,149 registered voters who either did not receive the previous mailing or who had registered to vote after the previous mailing.

For each phase, Handel's office sent three communications to the voters on the list. "The first piece," Handel recalled, "was a personal letter to the voter that said 'Important Voting Information Included.'" The office followed up with a brochure, and then a reminder postcard, each encouraging the voter to obtain photo identification. In addition to the direct voter contact, Handel's office continued to issue public service announcements on the radio, and also asked utility companies, phone companies, and cable companies to include voting information with their bills.

7 *Secretary of State Begins Phase 2 of Voter Outreach*, AccessNorthGA.com (Oct. 13, 2007), http://www.accessnorthga.com/detail.php?n=85067&c=10.

The entire effort cost Handel's office roughly $1.5 million, but Handel believes it was "money well spent." The implementation of the Georgia ID law, one of the strictest in the country, was, in Handel's view, "very smooth."

Just as Secretaries like Handel were called upon to educate their voters about identification requirements, those in other states, like Missouri Secretary Robin Carnahan, have sought to eliminate voter confusion about whether they would need ID in order to vote. In 2006, the Missouri legislature enacted a law that required all voters to produce a government-issued photo ID prior to voting. Carnahan immediately developed a photo ID awareness initiative to inform Missouri voters about the new requirement, called the "Show Your Face at the Polls" campaign. At the time, Carnahan estimated that roughly 200,000 voting-age Missourians lacked adequate identification and announced her intentions to spend $3.5 million to educate voters about the requirement.

But shortly before Election Day in 2006, the Missouri Supreme Court struck down the law as a violation of the state's constitution.[8] Many voters—and poll workers—were left confused. Ironically, when Secretary Carnahan attempted to vote in person in November 2006, a poll worker asked to see her ID. Carnahan recalls that when she explained that the law did not require her to produce identification, the poll worker told her, "We know it's not the law, but we've been told to ask for it anyway."

"To have that experience personally was very troubling," Carnahan said to a reporter after the incident occurred. She declared: "I want to make sure that voters are clear, that election authorities are clear," that there was no photo identification requirement in Missouri.[9]

The Secretary as Educator: Building an Educated Electorate

Apart from work to educate voters on the mechanics of voting, several secretaries go beyond this initial responsibility, they make it a priority to build an educated electorate. Through specific voter information guides that provide balanced details about candidates and ballot initiatives, or through extensive and broad voter education efforts that seek to develop an informed and engaged citizenry. Former Oregon Secretary of State Bill Bradbury published a voter guide in 2008 that provided extensive and objective information on each of the candidates running for office and ballot proposals, which he posted online and mailed to every household.[10] Bradbury's office also published an annual synopsis of all changes to election law, to assist voters in staying up to date on all new voting procedures.

8 See *Weinschenk v. State*, 203 S.W.3d 201 (Mo. 2006).

9 *Secretary of State Complains about Confusion over ID*, Columbia Tribune, Nov. 7, 2006, available at: http://archive.columbiatribune.com/2006/nov/20061107news013.asp (accessed Aug. 22, 2009).

10 Oregon Secretary of State online Voter Guide for Nov. 4, 2008, available at: http://www.sos.state.or.us/elections/nov42008/guide/cover.html (accessed Aug. 22, 2009).

California Secretary Debra Bowen provides a downloadable audio version of her office's official voter information guide.[11] In addition to providing information on registering to vote, voting by mail, provisional balloting, finding a polling place, and becoming a poll worker, the guide includes the full text of each ballot proposal, including arguments for and against and an analysis of each from a nonpartisan Legislative Analyst. The guide is available online in several languages, including Chinese, Japanese, Korean, Spanish, Tagalog, and Vietnamese.

Washington Secretary Sam Reed's "number one priority" when he became Secretary was to ensure the office made improvements to provide educational information to the voters regarding candidates and issues. Reed was initially deterred from implementing these educational goals by a lawsuit challenging the state's "top two" primary system, which allows the top two vote getters in a primary to face off in a general election, regardless of their party affiliation. Reed's office sent a written voters' pamphlet to every household in the state, as well as developed an electronic voters' pamphlet, and a video voters' guide. The extensive Voter Guide and other information, available at http://www.secstate.wa.gov/elections, enables voters in the state of Washington to go to the website, enter their name and their birth date, and learn about candidates and initiatives. Reed's system, called "My Vote," includes information on school district board members, county commissioners, city councils, legislators, and members of Congress.

Several Secretaries implement voter and civic education programs for young citizens—like Kansas Secretary Ron Thornburgh's Kids Voting Kansas program, which seeks to educate Kansas youth about the rights, responsibilities, and mechanics of participation in American democracy. In Rhode Island, Secretary Ralph Mollis created RI VOTE!, a statewide, grassroots voter education and outreach program developed during the November 2004 elections with initiatives directed to military voters (RI Troops Vote!), first time voters (First Voters!), and youth (Youth Vote!).

Vermont Secretary Deb Markowitz participates in a high school registration week by registering eligible high school students and speaking to civics education classes. She also created the Vermont Votes for Kids program in 2003, which allowed kindergarten to grade twelve students to take a lesson on voting and then cast their ballots alongside eligible voters on Election Day. The program expanded to all schools in 2004, when Markowitz's office also developed an online multidisciplinary curriculum to help students learn how to research candidates.

Arkansas Secretary Charlie Daniels hosts a young voter education program twice each year, which includes a mock election, a review of the history of voting rights in America, information on the state's high school poll worker program, and a discussion on civil rights. Eligible young citizens are then invited to register to vote at the end of the program. Similarly, Secretary Jennifer Brunner created

11 California Official Voter Information Guide, available at: http://www.voterguide.sos.ca.gov/audio/ (accessed Aug. 22, 2009).

"Grads Vote 2008," which distributed voter registration packets with all high school diplomas, reaching approximately 145,000 graduating high school seniors in 2008. In Washington, the Secretary sponsors a mock election for all students in grades kindergarten to twelve and sends voter registration forms to all Washington citizens on their eighteenth birthday.

In Louisiana, Secretary of State Jay Dardenne created "Geaux Vote" in 2008. In addition to traditional voter education information, "Geaux Vote" included a program called "The Road to the White House." This, according to Dardenne, was an "educational program that enabled students to track the presidential campaign, [from] the primaries and caucuses, all the way through to the election." Dardenne's program did not provide any data on candidates or their platforms, but instead provided "a blueprint for students to do their own research and enter it into a journal in order to follow the election." The computer-based journal-like program enabled users to enter, view, and print information that they were able to find through their own research, giving voters the tools to develop their candidate analysis. The program also included a corresponding curriculum for educators to incorporate into their classrooms.

Iowa Secretary of State Michael Mauro oversees the AIM Program, which seeks to provide information on voting and the democratic process, and mentoring programs for youth. AIM specifically incorporates Advocating Change Day and Capitol Youth Day. Advocating Change Day is a day designated for people with disabilities and their families to visit the State Capitol and learn how to communicate with legislators effectively. Capitol Youth Day is an annual event at the State Capitol for students in grades six to twelve. It allows students the opportunity to visit the State Capitol and meet statewide elected officials and legislators. Students also explore the workings of the legislative process by learning how to draft bills and participating in a mock legislative debate.

Similarly, Nebraska Secretary John Gale oversees several civic education events geared towards young people, including Nebraska Student Vote and the Youth Election Service. The Youth Election Service ("YES") offers Nebraska students a $50 savings bond for working or volunteering with election officials on election day. The Nebraska Student Vote is a program designed for grades kindergarten through twelve that combines civics instruction with a mock election. To Gale, these programs are an example of his work to be "aggressive and proactive about voter education and citizen outreach." Gale sees his role as being a "cheerleader to encourage good citizenship." Gale's office also sponsors a statewide birthday party every year, Statehood Day, during which his office travels 1,200 miles over the course of five days, to "celebrate citizenship and Nebraska statehood, state pride, [and] civic pride." Gale estimates that he "entertained over 25,000 fourth graders" in his first seven years as Nebraska Secretary of State. But to Gale, his motivation is drawn from a need to "lay the foundation early with young people to be proud to be citizens, proud to be Americans, proud of their history, proud of their patriotism."

With all that Gale has implemented in Nebraska, Kentucky Secretary Trey Grayson of Kentucky has set the bar even higher. In his first term as Secretary of State, Grayson developed one of the most extensive and comprehensive civics education programs in the country. The Civic Literacy Initiative of Kentucky (CLIK), formalized under a 2004 joint resolution by the Kentucky General Assembly, is a nonpartisan multi-year effort to increase civic literacy and engagement throughout the state.

In 2004 Grayson convened the Kentucky Summit on Civic Literacy at Northern Kentucky University. The Summit included 170 participants from across the state, including students, elected officials, community leaders, and educators, who convened to discuss ways to improve the civic engagement of the state's citizens. Eleven regional summits, held throughout the state, followed the 2004 statewide summit, and the state sponsored a second statewide summit in 2005. Out of the summits emerged the report, *Rediscovering Democracy: An Agenda for Action*. The report's sixty recommendations focus on four areas: civic education resources, civic programs and curriculum, professional development, and standards and assessment. Its key suggestions were (1) the establishment of a Kentucky Center for Civic Excellence to provide a central location to house civic knowledge, data, and resources; (2) the creation of a pilot study of a high school government and civics course that integrates information on civic literacy and civic engagement at the local, state, and federal level; (3) the creation of an annual teacher academy and network to provide professional development for educators in the area of government and civics; and (4) increasing the degree to which government and civics are assessed in the blueprint of the statewide student assessment.[12]

Since the release of the report, Grayson's office has been at the forefront of advocating for legislation to implement these recommendations. In consultation with the University of Louisville, he has implemented a pilot study of the development of a high school government and civics course that would integrate civic literacy and engagement at the local, state, and federal level, including the development of innovative ways to incorporate civics into other subject areas such as science, math, and reading. His office collaborated with the Kentucky Department of Education to create an annual teacher academy to provide professional development for educators in the area of government and civics. This also includes an on-line forum for teachers to share ideas. Most significantly, Grayson's effort led to a 5 percent increase in the measurement of government and civics in Kentucky's statewide student assessment.

12 The entire report is available at: http://civics.ky.gov/NR/rdonlyres/ADE310B9-48E2-4DEC-990D-E9E332E1E98B/0/RDA.pdf (accessed Aug. 22, 2009).

Educating Local Election Administrators

The role of the Secretary of State as the state's chief educator on voting and election law does not end with the voter. Most Secretaries also take seriously the need to ensure that all local election administrators—from clerks to poll workers—are continuously and accurately informed of all election laws and procedures.

In order to avoid the types of problems Secretary Carnahan dealt with when she was wrongly asked to provide photo identification before voting in a Missouri election, it is crucial that all local election authorities are aware of and comply with state and federal law. Many Secretaries take a hands-on approach to this challenge, overseeing the development and implementation of comprehensive mandatory training programs for clerks and poll workers. Kansas Secretary Ron Thornburgh believes that election security which "involves voter registration, tabulation, ballot creation, programming, officials themselves … is driven at the polling place on election day," Kansas Secretary Ron Thornburgh prioritizes the need to ensure "well trained poll workers, [and] well trained election officials." Thornburgh's office conducts an "extensive training of county election officers through a certification program, a three year education program for county clerks." Beyond that, his office requires "eight hours of training per year for elections officials and their deputies. "We very aggressively train them and they very aggressively in turn train their poll workers," he notes.

In March 2008, just before the state's June presidential primary, North Dakota Secretary Al Jaeger held a two-day elections conference to provide local elections officials with the opportunity to brush up on new voting laws and procedures. Of particular importance for Jaeger was vote-by-mail procedures, since nearly half of his state's counties would implement it that year.

Vermont Secretary Deb Markowitz is an attorney with a background in municipal and local government law. In the months leading up to an election, Markowitz personally trains town clerks and other elections officials on election procedures and guidelines. "In my experience" Markowitz noted, "our clerks want to be able to call someone who knows more than they do. It is a tremendous asset that I am an attorney, but I am also an educator." While Vermont law requires Markowitz to organize regional training sessions for election officials, Markowitz chose to conduct most training herself "because I love going out there working with the clerks and the elections officials. … [I]t's about an hour and a half training we do, what they need to do to run the elections and that's really gratifying."

In conducting the training, Markowitz works to familiarize election workers with new laws, including, in 2008, new regulations that set a voter registration deadline of 5 p.m. on the Wednesday before the election and allowed polling places to open at 5 a.m. She also seeks to address problems that resulted in complaints to her office in recent elections, including complaints of election officials standing too close to voters as they complete and submit their ballots, and problems with the state's vote-by-telephone system.

New Mexico Secretary Mary Herrera oversees thirty-three county clerks. After her election in 2006 Herrera, a former county clerk herself, made it a priority to ensure training sessions held before every primary and general election, were thorough and accurate. Among other things, she asked the U.S. Post Office to send officials to the training to discuss ways to ensure the accurate and secure handling of all absentee ballots. She also brought in vendors who print ballots and test and fix all of the voting equipment to discuss the machines and review techniques for troubleshooting. Her training curriculum included instructions on handling challengers and observers. Notably, she included audits on reported problems in each county in recent elections to discuss and minimize the potential for recurring problems. Following her first training session, a Republican clerk approached Herrera, a Democrat, and told her that "this has been one of the best trainings we've received in ten years." As a former county clerk, Herrera "knew what was lacking and what was needed" and thus "made sure we covered everything that we could possibly think of that will help our county clerks run a smoother election."

Beyond training of election officials, many Secretaries, like Herrera have worked to ensure consistent poll worker training throughout their states. To Georgia Secretary Karen Handel, one of the most important aspects of her effort to ensure the smooth implementation of her state's photo identification requirement for voters was poll worker training. To Handel,

> "It was important that poll workers know precisely what to do if the individual did not have one of the required forms of photo identification, and the right thing to do, and this came from my lips to every county elections officials' ears. If in doubt, you always issue a provisional ballot. No person should walk away from a precinct without at least having been able to vote a provisional ballot, because that is the right thing to do when you're talking about a person's ability to vote."

Like Brunner, Mauro, and Ireland, Handel's office implemented an online training module on the new photo identification program for poll workers to supplement in-person training in the counties. Prior to the development of the online module, Handel noted that Georgia's 159 county officials "had 159 different ways of doing poll worker training." Handel believed, "in order for something to ultimately be successful, you need to have consistency and uniformity. And the only way to get that was to have one training module." Though in Georgia it remains the job of the local clerk "to actually be the front line trainer for poll workers," they partner with Secretary Handel's office to ensure that all training programs provide accurate and reliable information.

In New Mexico, Herrera developed an instructional guide and accompanying video that must be shown at each training session. The video specifically reviews "opening of the polls, closing of the polls, what is a provisional ballot, … equipment, [and] how to treat people with disabilities." Herrera also created a system to educate voters about the state's voter identification requirement, which does not require that voters present photo identification, but does require that they give their name, address, and year of birth. In previous elections the posting of such information was voluntary and thus sporadic throughout the state, Herrera issued a directive requiring all clerks to post the information in a visible location for all voters to see and review.

Other Secretaries have attempted similar innovations to ensure that all poll workers in their state are trained consistently and accurately. Nevada Secretary Ross Miller noted the importance of ensuring consistent poll worker training. In his state, "Some of our counties do a better job of it than others." The variation typically depends on the wealth and resources of the particular county. Miller's office seeks to fill in gaps in counties with fewer resources through the development of best practices manuals and statewide poll worker recruitment methods. Betty Ireland, former Secretary for West Virginia, partnered with Marshall University to create a statewide poll worker training program that her office implemented via online poll worker training videos.

In Ohio, Secretary Jennifer Brunner implemented an online poll worker training program that is free and voluntary, but which seeks to provide a "uniform supplement" to current local training programs. Brunner also developed a "Quick Reminder List" and a printed poll worker manual for workers in all counties. Iowa Secretary Michael Mauro is also developing a similar online training program, and has implemented a statewide training and certification program for its poll workers, a three day program that has certified over 2,000 poll workers throughout the state.

California Secretary Debra Bowen created a Task Force on Uniform Poll Worker Training Standards to help her office ensure that her state's poll workers were properly and accurately trained. Bowen's office also has an optional online test for poll workers, which highlights basic legal issues. Her office also observes poll worker training and polling place operations on Election Day to provide feedback to localities on needed improvements to their poll worker training program. Through this observation she learned of "issues in the February [presidential] primary with some poll workers not giving voters, who declined to state an affiliation with a political party [on their voter registration form], the party ballot that they requested." Bowen's online self-test subsequently emphasized that legal requirement. She also explored the potential recruitment of election attorneys to conduct poll worker training sessions for counties throughout her state.

Conclusion

What is quickly apparent after a survey of the different ways in which a Secretary serves as "Elections Educator," is that the role can be as big—or as small—as a Secretary makes it. The above examples illustrate several recent innovative approaches Secretaries have pursued in taking an expansive approach to the role. This can involve programs ranging from disseminating information to voters on the mechanics of voting, providing substantive voting guides that detail candidates and ballot initiatives, training and educating local election officials, and reforming the entire system of civics education in their state.

Because Secretaries work statewide, these expansive approaches not only ensure that their state has more educated democratic actors. Their educational efforts, like Handel's in Georgia, also enable uniform interpretations and understanding of the law. Statewide educational campaigns can come close to eliminating confusion about voting among citizens, poll workers, and local election administrators while ensuring that the understanding that emerges is uniform and consistent.

This enhanced evenhanded and collective understanding of democratic rights and responsibilities leads to a better application of the constitutional principles of equal protection and one person, one vote. The fact, as the above examples illustrate, that Secretaries can play such a central role in developing educational programs that have this far-reaching effect of furthering these constitutional goals makes their role crucial indeed.

Kentucky Secretary of State
Trey Grayson

First Elected: 2002

Trey Grayson was just thirty-one years old when he was elected Kentucky's Secretary of State in 2002, making him the youngest Secretary of State in the country at the time. Grayson has used his youth to his advantage, building a strong base of support among college students and young professionals, promoting his candidacy via new media outlets such as Facebook and MySpace. He also updated his office's website to include numerous online resources, while making it available in six different languages.

Grayson has truly used his pulpit as Secretary in ways that go beyond traditional work. He has become a national voice advocating for reform to the political parties' system of conducting presidential primaries. And he's promoted a multi-state verification system of voter registration to ensure that when citizens move and update their registration, their home states are able to remove the former residents and keep their rolls accurate. Grayson has also developed an eighty-five page manual on running for office called "Declaring Your Candidacy," demystifying the process for those with an interest in becoming elected public servants.

But the centerpiece of Grayson's work as Secretary has been his innovative efforts at improving civic literacy and political engagement in his state. Since taking office, he has spearheaded reforms in his state that include: a pilot study of a high school government and civics course that integrates civic literacy and civic engagement at the local, state, and federal level, an annual teacher academy and network to provide professional development in the area of government and civics, advocating for the establishment of a Kentucky Center for Civic Excellence in partnership with state universities or colleges, and increased the degree to which government and civics are assessed in the blueprint of the statewide student assessment.

Grayson's youth and energy helped enable him to take his office in innovative new directions, becoming a model for other Secretaries who seek to promote democratic values in unique ways.

Chapter 6
The Secretary as Election Reformer

> "One of the big challenges in government is that you don't get new people and fresh ideas. Institutional knowledge is great, but if that's all you have, you lose innovation and get mired in the status quo. I think all of the Secretaries of State, when it comes to election reform, have tremendous opportunity to influence the process, whether it be through policy making or through the legislative process."
>
> Georgia Secretary of State Karen Handel

In 1972, Bill Gardner and several other young twenty-somethings were elected to serve in the New Hampshire state legislature. At the time Gardner was elected, on the eve of Watergate, election reform was on the minds of many of his colleagues in the legislature. As a state legislator, Gardner developed a series of proposals to improve election administration in New Hampshire, following a particularly controversial election. One reform was a policy to protect the security of paper ballots through improving procedures for handling the ballots. But Legislator Gardner's proposals were rejected across the board. None were successfully enacted into law.

A few years later, in the December of 1976, a vote of the legislature (the body that elects the New Hampshire Secretary of State) led to Gardner's election to the office. In his first term as Secretary, Gardner re-submitted all of his election reform proposals that the state legislature had rejected a few years earlier. Now championed by a sitting Secretary, nearly every proposal passed.

Similarly, soon after Michael Mauro's election as Iowa Secretary of State in 2006, he successfully led an effort to enact a law to allow voters to register to vote when they arrived at the polls on Election Day. Initially, Mauro noted, it was an uphill battle. "I approached the legislature with the idea of Election Day Registration and they were apprehensive about how we were going to administer this." Mauro built a team that visited election officials in states like Minnesota and Wisconsin to develop the provision. He recalls: "We had to work really hard at it. We went and visited Minnesota and we went and visited a couple of other states, Wisconsin, and we put some good [safeguards] into the law … [in order to] significantly help the comfort level with some of the people out there who are worried about [voter impersonation]."

His success, Mauro believes, can be partially attributed to the fact that when he "came into the office of Secretary of State, it was with the right intentions." Mauro explained:

> "one of the funny things that was said on the campaign trail was that I might be one of the few people that in the whole country who is running for secretary of state who actually wants to be secretary of state. … I wanted to be the secretary of state, I wanted to do the right thing for the election process and I think that helped me tremendously."

Mauro and Gardner's experiences epitomize the unique vantage point, bully pulpit, and credible authority that accompanies being the state's chief elections official. Secretaries of State are able to identify and advocate for reforms to the elections process with an authority that few other figures possess. And in recent years, particularly following the 2000 presidential elections, Secretaries have led to the improvement of election law in several states. To Georgia Secretary Karen Handel, who has made election reform a central theme of her administration, "the Secretary of State's role is the policy making aspect of elections. We set the broad policies for the conduct of elections." Likewise, when Vermont Secretary Markowitz entered office immediately following the 2000 presidential election, she devised and advocated for a package of election reforms "designed to update [Vermont] laws that were really in need of freshening." Markowitz found that "there were a lot of laws on the books that no longer were being followed, [and that] were outdated, and there was a lot of unnecessary bureaucracy that made it more difficult for voters, administrators, and more difficult for candidates to get on the ballot. So we did a general freshening of the statutes."

Collaboration and cooperation are key to the development of these policies. Many Secretaries form commissions, task forces, or other types of committees to advise or inform their efforts. Seeking to encourage civic engagement among Nebraska college students, Secretary John Gale formed a College Student Advisory Committee, with representatives from three University of Nebraska campuses. Gale formed a broader election reform task force with state legislators in 2003, and also joined a multi-state initiative with Secretaries Mauro in Iowa, Thornburgh in Kansas, and Carnahan in Missouri to develop methods for improving voter registration and the training of elections officials. In 2003, Vermont Secretary Deborah Markowitz, Indiana Secretary Todd Rokita, and Arizona Secretary Jan Brewer were among those who convened advisory committees in the respective states, comprised of election clerks, nonpartisan nonprofit representatives, and state legislators, to assist with the implementation of the Help America Vote Act (HAVA).

Out of these commissions and other efforts often emerge legislative packages or bundled reforms that Secretaries either seek to implement independently under the authority of their office, or champion through their state legislative branch. Secretary Gale's election reform committee, for example, produced a legislative package that was signed into law and, among other things, permitted all rural counties to hold their elections by mail, allowed for early voting, and provided for the voting rights for the children of servicemen and servicewomen who are born overseas, but whose parents are registered to vote in Nebraska.

Of that package, Gale is most proud of his successful advocacy for mail voting for rural counties. He explained that from his office, he observed the population of rural Nebraska declining, requiring a reduction of precincts in those areas of his state. And "in that process," Gale

> "realized that some of these new precincts we created were very, very large and the farmers and ranchers in those areas were going to have to travel fairly long distances on country roads in order to vote, if we required them to show up and vote at a precinct. We realized that that's not practical nor is it safe to require that of our rural population."

Using his office to advocate for reforms that would serve this population, Gale worked with members of the Nebraska legislature to pass a law that would allow counties that have less than 7,000 citizens to apply to the Secretary of State's office for permission to switch to all-mail voting in certain precincts. Gale recalled that he "thought it might be controversial but actually the senators from the rural areas were very supportive of the idea." And while the Nebraska legislature "did not want us to become an all mail-in state, like Oregon, they realized that in order to assure a continuing good turnout of voters and to take weather and safety" into consideration, "they had to allow for this reform."

As these stories illustrate, the successful passage of these reforms is often times chiefly due to the advocacy of the state's chief elections official. In Iowa, Secretary of State Michael Mauro was heralded as "one of the big winners at the statehouse" in 2008, after Iowa lawmakers from both political parties supported and enacted several of his election law reforms. Remarking on Mauro's success, one State Representative noted that Mauro "really put himself on the line, spent a lot of time with us in working through those bills and trying to get people on board."[1] Similarly, Gale felt his success in getting his legislative reforms through the Nebraska legislature could be directly attributed to his energetic advocacy.

The Secretary and Voter Identification

In 2003, Indiana Secretary Todd Rokita developed a "Vote Indiana Team" to develop a plan for improving Indiana's elections process. According to Rokita, the "Team," which consisted of individuals representing "three political parties, the state legislature, minority groups, military voters, people with disabilities, county election and voter registration officials, and the media," was charged with developing a plan to implement the Help America Vote Act and for modernizing the state's elections process. After many of the "Team's" recommendations formed the basis of the

1 O. Kay Henderson, *Secretary of State Big Winner in '08 Session*, Radio Iowa News, April 26, 2008, http://www.radioiowa.com/gestalt/go.cfm?objectid=87365268-99A5-FC76-808ADA39F9D4F044 (accessed Aug. 22, 2009).

passage for several pieces of legislation, Rokita formed a more specific "Vote with ID Task Force" to develop a proposal and implementation plan for requiring voters to present photo identification when arriving at the polls on Election Day.

Rokita calls his subsequent successful advocacy for enacting Indiana's photo identification requirement his "claim to fame." "When I ran for office," he explained,

> "photo ID at the polls was part of my platform. And the idea was: people are cheating. And where I came down on it, was whether you believe that voter fraud exists or not, this introduces a level of confidence for the voter. And if people thought that ok, these people at the polling places are doing at least the same kind of thing that the 18 year old does at the video store or the bank, I'm going to invest my time in it again, I'm going to sit for 20 minutes in line because I know some checks that are done in the rest of society are done here at the polling place."

It is important to couch Rokita's contributions to the development of identification requirements for voters in the larger context of the evolution of those requirements across the country. Secretaries of State have been at the forefront of advocating for, fighting against, and administering identification requirements for voters over the past decade. Missouri Secretary Robin Carnahan, for example, believes that a photo ID requirement would stop election fraud only in rare cases where someone tries to impersonate another voter at the polls, and has emphasized that "[w]e have found no documented instances of voter impersonation in our state." Missouri's photo ID law was struck down in 2006 by the state Supreme Court, which found the requirement placed too great a burden on the right to vote. The court found that as many as 240,000 registered voters in the state did not have the necessary ID and might be discouraged from going through the red tape and costs of obtaining documents such as birth certificates.

And in 2007, after the Michigan State Supreme Court issued an opinion activating the state's dormant identification requirement,[2] Michigan Secretary

2 The Michigan voter photo identification law was initially enacted in 1996 and subsequently deemed unconstitutional by then-state Attorney General Frank Kelley. On July 18, 2007, however, the state Supreme Court overruled the Attorney General's ten-year-old opinion and deemed the requirement to be "facially constitutional." The court found the identification requirement to be a "reasonable, nondiscriminatory restriction designed to preserve the purity of elections and to prevent abuses of the electoral franchise, as demanded by art 2, § 4 of the Michigan Constitution, thereby preventing lawful voters from having their votes diluted by those cast by fraudulent voters." The Michigan law mandates that each individual voting in person on Election Day present a driver's license, state-issued photo identification, "or other generally recognized picture identification card." Under the text of the law, if a voter is unable to present an acceptable piece of photo identification, they are permitted to "sign an affidavit … and be allowed to vote" but are "subject to challenge" by any observing individual who has "good cause" to do so.

of State Terry Lynn Land issued a set of regulations that instituted enforceable clarifications to guide the local implementation of the law.[3] These regulations,[4] offered a limited definition of "generally recognized picture identification card" that did not include, for example, photo identification issued by an employer, or a credit or ATM card with a photo,[5] both of which are acceptable forms of identification under Michigan's interpretation of HAVA.[6] In addition, nowhere in the instructions are poll workers instructed to resolve doubts as to a voter's identity in favor of the voter, inviting reliance on subjective perceptions of poll workers as to whether a voter's photograph clearly resembles the voter. According to Secretary Land's guidelines, a voter may be directed to cast a provisional ballot if a poll worker does not believe that the photo in the identification card resembles the voter.

All Secretaries were required to consider the implementation of voter identification requirements after Congress created a federal identification provision in the Help America Vote Act (HAVA) in 2002. HAVA requires all voters who register to vote by mail and vote in person in their first election provide some form of acceptable identification when they arrive at the polls to vote.[7] The federal law allows voters to present either a copy of 'a current and valid photo identification' or 'a copy of a current utility bill, bank statement, government check, paycheck, or other government document that shows the name and address of the voter."[8] In addition, any voter who is required to show identification under HAVA and is unable to do so when they show up to vote is entitled under the law to cast

---

3 See *Picture Identification at the Polls: Instructions to Election Officials*, Michigan Department of State, available at: http://www.michigan.gov/documents/sos/090507_Voter_Id_QA5_209294_7.pdf (accessed Aug. 22, 2009).

4 The lack of any opportunity for the public to weigh in and comment on the Secretary of State's development of regulations is arguably in violation of Michigan law. MCL 168.31 (1) (a) requires the Secretary of State to "issue instructions and promulgate rules pursuant to the [Michigan] administrative procedures act ... for the conduct of elections and registrations in accordance with the laws of this state." The Michigan APA requires state agencies to give notice and opportunity for comment prior to promulgating any "agency regulation, statement, standard, policy, ruling, or instruction of general applicability that implements or applies law enforced or administered by the agency, or that prescribes the organization, procedure, or practice of the agency, including the amendment, suspension, or rescission of the law enforced or administered by the agency." MCL 24.207.

5 In addition to a driver's license or state-issued photo identification, Michigan voters under the Secretary's regulations could present a driver's license or personal identification card with photo from any state or the federal government, a passport, student ID with a photo from a high school or other accredited school, a military ID, or tribal identification.

6 *Procedure for Implementing Federal Identification Requirement in Polls*, Michigan Dept. of State, http://www.michigan.gov/documents/Fed_ID_Req_105890_7.pdf (accessed Aug. 22, 2009).

7 Help America Vote Act of 2002, 42 U.S.C.A. 15483 (2006).

8 Help America Vote Act of 2002, 42 U.S.C.A. 15483(b)(2)(A)(i).

a provisional ballot,[9] to be counted at a later time if some circumstance is met. HAVA's section on when to count provisional ballots, however, does not indicate what a voter who does not present acceptable identification is required to do or provide in order to ensure their vote is counted.[10]

Beyond those terms, the determination of what comprises "current and valid" photo identification or "other government document" is left to the states and, usually, the state Secretary of State. Law Professor and Director of Ohio State's Election Reform Center Dan Tokaji notes that as a result Secretaries can be confronted with numerous questions: "Should a student ID, for example, suffice? What about a bus pass? ... If a student is enrolled at a public university, will a printout from the registrar's office showing her address suffice?"[11]

This lack of specificity in HAVA's identification requirements implicitly grants discretion to states in determining how to administer and enforce the law, as well as how to publicize its requirements. This deference leads to one of two outcomes, both of which implicate the Secretary of State. The state legislature, particularly when enacting legislation to adopt HAVA's requirements for their state elections, could enact its own legislation to fill the void by providing a long list of acceptable identifications and instructions as to how the provisional ballot "safety net" should be addressed.[12] Or, the state legislature could, like Congress, offer little to no detailed directives for implementing the new requirements. And in both situations, the Secretary of State is charged (or left) with providing answers to any and all questions left unanswered and ensuring that she, the local clerks, and the voters are prepared for all possible Election Day scenarios.

California, for example, enacted legislation that permits items ranging from "an ID card provided by a commercial establishment" to "a lease or rental statement or agreement" to a doctor's prescription with the voter's name and address to suffice as proper identification.[13] The law further requires that "any doubts regarding the

9 42 U.S.C.S. § 15483(2)(b)(i) ("an individual who desires to vote in person, but who does not meet the requirements of subparagraph (A)(i), may cast a provisional ballot under section 302(a)").

10 Daniel P. Tokaji, *Symposium: Early Returns on Election Reform: Discretion, Disenfranchisement, and the Help America Vote Act*, 73 Geo. Wash. L. Rev. 1206, 1234 (describing this problem in greater detail).

11 *Id.* at 1233.

12 For example, California's state election code includes a laundry list of acceptable forms of voter identification. See 2 CCR 20107 (2006).

13 See 2 CCR 20107 (the full list includes: a driver's license of any state, a passport, an employee ID card, an ID card provided by a commercial establishment, a credit or debit card, a military ID card, a student ID card, a health club ID card, an insurance plan ID card, utility bill, bank statement, government check, government paycheck, any document issued by a governmental agency with a voter's name and address, a voter notification card; a public housing ID card, a lease or rental statement or agreement, a tuition statement or bill, discharge certificates, pardons, or other official documents issued to the voter in connection with the resolution of a criminal case, indictment, sentence, or other matter,

sufficiency of identification presented shall be resolved in favor of the voter."[14] The law also allows for the Secretary of State to permit "any other document specified in writing by the Secretary of State that includes the name and address of the individual presenting it, and is dated since the date of the last general election."[15] Thus though the list establishes a detailed baseline of acceptable documents, and there are many, it still allows the Secretary of State to develop an additional set of acceptable forms of identification.

Ohio took a different approach. The state assembly did not pass any legislation expanding or adding detail to the HAVA requirements prior to the 2004 election.[16] This meant that not only was the question of acceptable ID left vague and indistinct, but there was also no additional direction offered on how election administrators should evaluate any provisional ballots cast by voters without acceptable ID. In February 2004, then-Ohio Secretary of State Kenneth Blackwell sought to fill this void, announcing that provisional ballots cast by first time voters without proper ID would be counted only if the voters returned to the polling location and presented either a valid photo ID or other proof of name and address, or their driver's license number or the last four digits of their Social Security number, before the polls closed for the day.[17] After surviving a challenge in federal court,[18] this significant interpretative directive was enforced during the presidential election in Ohio in 2004.[19]

---

senior citizen discount cards issued by public transportation authorities, ID documents issued by government disability agencies, ID documents issued by government homeless shelters and other temporary or transitional facilities, drug prescription provided by a doctor or other health care provider, tax return, property tax statement, vehicle registration or certificate of ownership).

14 *Id.*

15 *Id.*

16 Tokaji, *supra* note 10, at 1233.

17 *Id.* (citing Directive No. 2004-07 from J. Kenneth Blackwell, Ohio Sec'y of State, to All County Boards of Elections Members, Directors, and Deputy Directors 3–4 (Feb. 20, 2004)).

18 *League of Women Voters v. Blackwell*, 340 F. Supp. 2d 823 (N.D. Ohio 2004).

19 Two years later, in 2006, the Ohio legislature enacted a state law that expanded the identification requirements in HAVA and required all voters to present some form of ID at the polls prior to voting. See ORC § 3505.18. The law requires all voters to provide proof of their identity, which can include "a current and valid photo identification, a military identification that shows the voter's name and current address, or a copy of a current utility bill, bank statement, government check, paycheck, or other government document, other than a notice of an election mailed by a board of elections … or a notice of voter registration mailed by a board of elections … that shows the name and current address of the elector." Voters arriving at the polls without such identification may cast a provisional ballot and now have ten days, under state law, to present the relevant identifying information or documents to the local election official. ORC §3505.18(2)-4. The Ohio Secretary of State has posted additional information on the requirements at: http://www.sos.state.oh.us/SOS/elections/voterInformation/bringid.aspx (accessed Aug. 22, 2009).

Blackwell focused on implementing identification requirements in an effort to advance electoral integrity, but he failed to balance those requirements with complementary efforts to encourage voter access and participation. He should have instituted additional regulations or advocated for new laws that would promote participation and access. Such laws could offset any limitations on access to voting that are indirectly caused through the new photo identification requirements.

For example, South Dakota Secretary Chris Nelson has overseen the implementation of a photo identification requirement in his state. But in response to an organization that was advocating for identification requirements, Nelson insisted that the group support no reason absentee voting as well, saying that "if we're going to do one, we're going to do the other." Implementing both at the same time, Nelson recognized, would ensure that a policy that promoted integrity but potentially limited access to the vote—the identification requirement—would be balanced with a policy—making it easier to cast an absentee ballot—that would promote access to the vote. His actions should be an example for other Secretaries seeking to recognize and balance various interests that underlie election reforms.

Beyond Legislative Reforms

In addition to championing reforms to their state's election laws, Secretaries are able to use their office in creative ways to develop, implement, or advocate for policies for such things as training and recruiting poll workers, maximizing the efficiency of precinct-level voting, and reforming the presidential primary process.

Because poll workers serve on the front lines of democracy on Election Day, many Secretaries work with local election officials to develop innovative reforms to the ways in which poll workers are recruited and trained. In 2008, then-Arizona Secretary Jan Brewer developed a "Corporate Challenge" program, getting businesses to encourage their employees to become poll workers through website announcements and inserts in their payroll checks. Brewer also asked companies to give their employees a day off work to serve as poll workers. Brewer's counterpart in Missouri, Secretary Robin Carnahan, built a statewide poll worker recruitment program that "reached across party lines" and was successful because of the universal recognition that "you have to have folks who know how to run the elections running the elections." She also used her office to spearhead a poll worker recruitment effort with several businesses in Missouri. In her view, serving as a poll worker is analogous to running a business where "voters are your customers, [and] nearly 3 million of your customers show up on the same day."

In Missouri, over 20,000 poll workers are needed to run a statewide election. Carnahan's recruitment initiatives identified more than 5,200 potential poll workers for local elections officials to appoint in their respective jurisdictions, including over 1,700 students. The focus on recruiting students grew out of a need for more poll workers, but also recognized that engaging young people to serve at the polls can contribute to their greater engagement in the electoral process. To Carnahan,

"There is nothing better students can do to learn about our great democracy than work side by side with our poll workers who have been participating for years."[20]

To assist in local efforts to hire and train more poll workers, Carnahan's office provided over $700,000 in grants to local election officials which were used to pay for more than half of the student poll workers statewide. In addition, while local election officials in Missouri are responsible for training their poll workers, Carnahan's office developed and provided materials to assist with training programs across the state. Carnahan also looked into whether individuals who served as poll workers could count that service as "jury duty," and thus be excused from serving on juries if they had worked as a poll worker. But she declined to pursue the idea after determining that it would reduce or potentially harm the pool of available jurors in her state.

Conclusion

Whether working on the state or local level, independently or in conjunction with state lawmakers, Secretaries of State have an unparalleled ability to advocate for improvements in the elections process is unparalleled. In particular, most Secretaries are able to use their rulemaking powers to develop either interpretations of existing law or new programs to facilitate improvements. In 2004, for example, former Missouri Secretary Matt Blunt made changes at the administrative levels of his office to improve Missourians' confidence in the election process. Among them: appointing, for the first time in state history, a Republican and Democratic Director of Elections and using the administrative rules process to define what constitutes a vote under Missouri's three voting systems, a major source of controversy in the disputed November 2000 election in Florida.

But to that end, many Secretaries were also quick to emphasize that their work alone was just one piece of a larger fabric of necessary components for reforms. For Kansas Secretary Ron Thornburgh and others, success comes through building relationships with the state legislature, but also collaborations with the general public. Thornburgh noted that he's been able to "effectively use the media to float some ideas" for reforms, which for him go a long way in building public involvement in improving the system of election administration.

The bottom line is that while Secretaries can and have utilized their position to wield significant influence as champions for reforms in the elections process, they cannot work alone. In the words of Vermont Secretary Deb Markowitz, "When you're talking about fundamental changes, it's got to come in part from the grassroots. It's not enough to be leading at the top if there are not people ready to jump in from the grassroots to be supportive." And collectively, from the top to roots, leaders can work with citizens to build a system that works for all.

20 Michael Sewall, *Grant Provides Extra Help for Student Poll Workers*, The Missourian, Aug. 5, 2008, http://www.columbiamissourian.com/stories/2008/08/05/grant-provides-extra-help-student-poll-workers/ (accessed Aug. 22, 2009).

Iowa Secretary of State
Michael Mauro

First Elected: 2006

When Michael Mauro ran for Secretary of State in 2006, he recalls, "One of the funny things said was that I might be one of the few people in the whole country who is running for Secretary of State who actually wants to be Secretary of State." A native of Iowa, he began his career as a high school teacher before working in the Polk County Auditor's Office where he rose through the ranks until reaching the position of auditor. He served as auditor for nine years before his election to Secretary of State in 2006.

During his tenure as Iowa Secretary of State, Mauro has worked hand-in-hand with the Iowa Legislature to establish same-day voter registration, making Iowa one of just a handful of states that allow voters to register to vote on Election Day. He attributes his success to his genuine commitment to making democracy work for every citizen in his state. "When I came into office," he notes, "I think I came in … with the right intentions and that was to be Secretary of State. I'm not here to toot my own horn. I want to do the right thing for the election process."

And to Mauro, allowing for same day registration was the right thing, despite the fact that in Iowa, he estimated that "about 90 or 92 percent of the total electorate" is already registered. "But I think we'll see," he noted, "people coming to the polling place on Election Day, new voters, 18 year olds registering for the first time, people who normally move from county to county coming in to register," to vote. Mauro's hope was that in November 2008, with the addition of the reform, Iowa's turnout would be one of the highest in the nation. And it was. In 2008, only five states had turnout higher than Iowa's, which came in at just over 70 percent.

Chapter 7
The Secretary and Voter Accessibility

> "There are groups that traditionally have not exercised the franchise at the same proportional level as the majority population. How do we ensure [their] access? How do I go about making sure that I provide for all, but make a particular effort towards those that we need to bring into the fold so that we have better participation?"
>
> Pennsylvania Secretary of State Pedro Cortés

A central tenet to the work of Secretaries charged with overseeing elections is promoting and enabling access to the political process. This tenet takes on a special challenge, however, in dealing with historically disenfranchised or otherwise uniquely situated communities.

Indeed, there are several groups of eligible voters who are uniquely situated and may require particular attention and proactive effort to ensure they enjoy equal access to the ballot box. Voters living or serving overseas, for example, do not enjoy the same ease of access to their local precinct, or even of receiving their absentee ballot, as those voters living within their state of residency. And voters with disabilities may require additional accommodation at the ballot box on Election Day to ensure their ballot is able to be cast and counted privately and accurately. Elderly voters, or citizens who are in the process of learning English, may also require additional services so that they may cast a fully informed vote.

The state Secretary of State has a special opportunity—and responsibility—to ensure, promote, and protect the political access of all uniquely situated voters. And around the country, many are developing innovative methods that go beyond state and federal legal requirements to achieve these goals. In order for these methods to be successful, however, it is crucial that Secretaries actively work with and involve community members when developing innovative techniques.

The Secretary and English-Learning Voters

One community of citizens who may encounter unique barriers when voting is that of citizens with limited English proficiency (LEP). These citizens are often native born, but raised in an environment where a language other than English is the dominant language. Or they may be naturalized citizens who emigrate from another country and begin developing fluency in English while living in the United States.

Either way, many citizens in LEP communities may be functionally fluent in English but may not be prepared to decipher complex ballot initiative language when casting their vote. For example, Senator Dianne Feinstein's mother, Betty Goldman, emigrated from Russia to the United States with her family at the age of four. She eventually learned to speak and write English and became a naturalized U.S. citizen. Her daughter grew up to become a United States Senator. But English was still Goldman's second language, and throughout her life, her daughter noted, she "could never really fully understand" complex ballot initiatives listed on the California ballot.

Fortunately for Goldman, her daughter and other family members were available to read and discuss the ballot with her. And many of the millions of United States citizens are afforded further accommodations under state and federal laws that seek to ensure that linguistic barriers do not stand in the way of their ability to exercise their fundamental right to vote with the same ease as any other citizen. Under federal law, Section 203 of the Voting Rights Act (the "Act") requires localities and states with high concentrations of Latino, Asian American, Native American, or Native Alaskan citizens to provide election materials in the native languages of those citizens.[1]

If a jurisdiction is covered under Section 203, the state or local jurisdiction must fund and provide election materials and assistance in the language of the applicable minority group. Beyond that, covered jurisdictions have a great deal of discretion as to how to comply with the provision. For example, states and jurisdictions may opt to use trained interpreters at poll sites and to "target" their assistance to certain areas or precincts for coverage. Federal regulations encourage jurisdictions to take appropriate steps to publicize the availability of translated materials, including the display of notices in the minority language, announcements over minority language radio or television stations, publication of notices in minority language newspapers, and direct contact with language minority group organizations.[2]

---

1 Specifically, under Section 203, any state or smaller jurisdiction (such as a county or parish) must provide language assistance if over 5 percent or more than 10,000 of the voting age citizens in the jurisdiction are members of a single covered language minority group and collectively have an illiteracy rate higher than the national average. The illiteracy rate is measured by the rate of the population over the age of twenty-five that has failed to complete the fifth grade. As interpreted by the U.S. Census Bureau in 2000, Section 203 accommodations extended to citizens of Chinese, Filipino, Japanese, Korean, Vietnamese, American Indian, and Native Alaskan descent. Section 203 was an expansion of another provision of the Voting Rights Act, Section 4(e), which was enacted in 1965. Section 4(e) prohibits discrimination against persons because of their "inability to read, write, understand, or interpret any matter in the English language," if they were educated through the sixth grade in an American school that delivered instruction in a language other than English. Although the provision led the way for the passage of Section 203 in 1975, it is generally interpreted to apply solely to citizens from Puerto Rico.

2 For a more detailed description of compliance problems, *see* Jocelyn F. Benson, *¡Su Voto Es Su Voz! Incorporating Voters of Limited English Proficiency into American*

Beyond these federal mandates, over thirty states have additional statutory requirements to accommodate voters with limited English proficiency. For example, state laws in California, Colorado, Maine, and Florida extend the coverage formula of Section 203 to require local jurisdictions to provide translated election materials. In California, LEP voters who live in a county that is not covered under Section 203 have the right to access a translated ballot and voting instructions in their native language, "if a significant and substantial need is found" by the local election official. California's laws also mandate that minority language sample ballots be provided and posted in polling areas where the Secretary of State determines that 3 percent or more of the voting age citizens are LEP, or when citizens or organizations provide information supporting a need for assistance. Local clerks are required under state law to make reasonable efforts to recruit election officials who are fluent in Spanish and other languages, and the Secretary of State's office provides voter information in seven languages, including English, Chinese, Korean, Spanish, Japanese, Tagalog, and Vietnamese. Florida's election accommodations are not as extensive, but similarly go beyond federal requirements by requiring the Secretary of State, upon the timely request of a local election official, to provide a written translation of a statewide ballot issue in any of the languages included under Section 203 of the Voting Rights Act.

In recent years, several Secretaries of State have gone beyond these state and federal statutory requirements to provide translated election material for English learning constituencies. Secretaries of State in several states, including Kansas, and Washington, voluntarily provide translated election material such as voter registration applications and absentee ballot request forms on their websites. The forms are provided in languages ranging from Spanish to Laotian to Russian to Bosnian. And in Iowa, until a lawsuit brought under his state's "English Only" law banned the practice, the Secretary of State proudly posted voter registration forms in various languages. Though Iowa Secretary Michael Mauro is no longer able to provide the forms, he remains a supporter of translated materials, emphasizing his belief that "the process should be open and it should be open to as many people as possible. I want people to participate, I want many people to participate, [and] I want to make it as easy as possible for them to do that at the same time [protecting] the security and integrity of the process."

Expanding on the need to proactively reach out to English-learning citizens beyond the provision of translated materials, Connecticut Secretary Susan Bysiewicz observed that the Latino community was a "community that is under-registered

---

Democracy, 48 B.C. L. Rev. 251 at 290 (2007) (describing "one infamous incident of poor compliance with section 203 … in New York City during the general election of 2000. On Election Day in Queens, Chinese language ballots were translated incorrectly at six voting sites, so that Democratic candidates were labeled as Republican, and Republican candidates were labeled as Democrats. During that same election, officials in Chinatown in Lower Manhattan scrambled to replace translated ballots that asked the voter to select five candidates for state supreme court justices when they were only permitted to select three").

and under-participates in elections in our state." So Bysiewicz implemented the 2008 '¡Tu Voto *Si* Cuenta!'—or, "Your vote *does* count!"—campaign to register 10,000 new Latino voters in Connecticut in time to participate in the November 2008 election. Bysiewicz emphasized that "as Connecticut's top elections official, I have always viewed one of my chief missions as encouraging more participation in the political process." She thus developed the program to communicate

> "to the more than 225,000 eligible Latino voters in Connecticut: your vote does count! Latinos are the largest and fastest growing ethnic group in our state and I believe we have an obligation to open the doors of democracy to everyone who is eligible to vote. That means reaching out to those who may feel left out and saying, we want to hear your voices too."

The campaign executed an "aggressive" media campaign to encourage voter participation, while providing, in Spanish, voter education materials explaining how to use paper ballots with the new optical scan voting technology, as well as information on voter rights and proper forms of identification for registering and voting.

The Secretary and the Disability Community

Another community of citizens who may benefit from accommodations when voting are citizens with disabilities. The types of accommodations needed, however, vary greatly based on the particular disability. They can range from making sure all polling places are accessible to individuals in wheelchairs to ensuring that there are machines available to assist visually impaired voters in casting their ballot.

As with LEP voters, federal law does provide some requirements to ensure that states provide voting access for citizens in these communities. In addition to providing funds to purchase new voting equipment and instituting an identification requirement for first-time voters, the 2002 Help America Vote Act (HAVA) also required that states upgrade and ensure access to voting for members of the disability community. Enacted in October 2002, HAVA specifically required that voting machines provide the "same opportunity for access and participation (including privacy and independence) as for other voters."[3] The law gave states three years—until January 1, 2006—to meet this requirement by providing at least one accessible voting system at each polling place.

Nearly every Secretary chose AutoMARK machines for meeting this requirement. The AutoMARK machines, designed to provide privacy and accessibility to voters who are vision-impaired, or have a disability or condition that would make it difficult or impossible to mark a paper ballot in the usual

3 42 U.S.C. § 15481(a)(3)(A) (2002).

way, are also able to be programmed to provide language assistance to voters who are more comfortable speaking in an alternative language or have reading limitations.

Part of the criticism of AutoMARK machines, however, is the lack of privacy inherent in the large screens they provide on which one can view and mark one's ballot. As a result, Maine Secretary Matt Dunlap didn't opt for AutoMARK machines. He explains,

> "[Y]ou have a right to vote, but you also have a right to a private vote. We spent a fair amount of money on public service announcements, getting the disabled community engaged, [a]nd I talked to some of those people and they said they had never been able to vote in private before, they always had someone mark their ballot and they didn't want people to know how they'd voted."

After consulting with a "broad range of interested individuals and organizations—including individuals with disabilities and local election officials," Secretary Dunlap used the HAVA funds to implement the "Inspire Vote-By-Phone system."[4] The system enables voters to cast their ballots from the precinct using a telephone. If a voter appears at the voting location and requests to vote by phone, the poll worker will then use the designated phone to call the central system, enter the appropriate access codes, and give the phone to the voter. After the voter receives audio instructions via the telephone, the voter can select their choices using the touch-pad on the phone. When the voter completes their ballot, they indicate that they have finished and the system transmits the voter's choices to a fax machine in the precinct. The voter then takes the paper ballot from the fax machine and runs it through the ballot counting machine.

Vermont Secretary Deb Markowitz and New Hampshire Secretary Bill Gardner also implemented the Vote-by-Phone system for physically-disabled and visually-impaired voters. Similar to Maine, the system provides a way for voters to cast their ballot by calling a special phone number that permits voters to mark a paper ballot using the telephone key pad. The ballot is printed out in the Elections Center, and is then counted with the rest of the ballots on Election Day. And like Dunlap, Markowitz developed the system in cooperation with a variety of disability groups, including the American Disability Association, the American Council for the Blind, and the National Federation for the Blind.

But even before HAVA funds became available, Markowitz worked to promote accessibility to voting for citizens with physical limitations. In 2001, Markowitz required all of Vermont's local elections officials to provide a report on accessibility of polling locations, including the location of the town's polling places, certifying that the polling places are accessible to voters with disabilities. If a polling place

---

4 *Press release: Secretary of State Matthew Dunlap Applauds Early Voting Pilot Project*, Maine Secretary of State, Oct. 31, 2007, http://maine.gov/sos/news/2007/EarlyVoting.html (accessed Aug. 22, 2009).

was not accessible, the clerk must provide documentation explaining why there are no accessible alternatives within the town and prove that it is not possible to make a site accessible before the next general election. Markowitz's goal was to ensure that by the general elections in November 2002, "each town in Vermont has added handicapped parking spaces, ramps, or have made other necessary improvements so that all polling places are accessible." Her office also provided each local elections official with a guide from the National Task Force on Accessible Elections that described the legal requirements and included practical suggestions for local election officials to improve accessibility.

And just before the 2004 election, Markowitz published a guide to poll workers on ensuring the proper treatment and accommodation of voters with disabilities. The brochure, entitled "Equal Access to Voting—It's the Law," included recommendations like "Use a normal voice when saying hello. Don't raise your voice unless requested." And "Do not automatically give assistance. Ask first if the person wants help. Many disabled people will be grateful for an offer of help. If your offer of assistance is accepted, listen to or ask for instructions."[5]

While Colorado Secretary Mike Coffman sought over $700,000 in federal funding throughout his tenure to similarly ensure adequate poll worker training on methods to promote access, another particularly innovative approach grew out of California Secretary Debra Bowen's office. Bowen commissioned the Voting Accessibility Advisory Committee (VAAC) to advise her on how best to provide resources for voters with disabilities. The VAAC was comprised of county elections officials and members of the disability community who have been involved in election-related issues and is charged with advising and providing recommendations to Bowen on the implementation of federal and state laws relating to access to the electoral process by voters with disabilities, so that all persons can vote independently and privately. The Committee's focus is specifically on developing accessibility guidelines for various aspects of the election administration process, including poll worker training on sensitivity to issues affecting the disability voting community.

Bowen also hosts an entire website dedicated to providing information on issues relating to voting and access for voters with physical limitation.[6] The website includes, among other things, a video in sign language on voting, a full brochure outlining the rights of voters with disabilities,[7] and a check list for evaluating

5 *Newly Published Guide Encourages People with Disabilities to Vote*, Vermont Secretary of State, Oct. 27, 2004, http://www.sec.state.vt.us/secdesk/pressreleases/2004/October04.html#PRESS%20RELEASE%203 (accessed Aug. 22, 2009).

6 *Voters with Disabilities—Know Your Rights*, California Secretary of State, available at: http://www.sos.ca.gov/elections/elections_dis.htm (accessed Aug. 22, 2009).

7 *Your Voting Rights: A Guide for Voters With Disabilities*, California Secretary of State, May 2008, http://www.sos.ca.gov/elections/election_2008/voting_rights_may_08.pdf (accessed Aug. 22, 2009).

whether California polling places are accessible to voters with disabilities.[8] The website also includes a "suggestion box" that enables any citizen to send email comments with ideas on how to improve accessibility.

The Secretary and Voters Serving or Living Overseas

Beyond citizens living on American soil, those who are serving in the military or living abroad for other reasons also encounter unique challenges in seeking to cast their ballot. It can be difficult to nearly impossible for citizens serving in the military in particular, sometimes even deployed to combat zones on Election Day, to ensure their absentee ballot is requested and received on time.

As with LEP citizens and citizens with physical disabilities, there are some federal statutory mandates in place to ensure states recognize and accommodate these uniquely situated voters. Under the Federal Uniformed and Overseas Citizens Absentee Voting Act (UOCAVA) of 1986 (42 USC 1973ff), all states and territories must provide mechanisms for U.S. citizens living or serving abroad to register and vote in elections for federal office by mail.

But requiring vote by mail has not been without its problems, and it is not unusual for registration forms, ballot request forms, or ballots themselves to get lost en route to or from the mailing elections official.[9] According to a 2006 study commissioned by the United States Elections Assistance Commission, roughly about a third of all absentee ballots requested by those serving abroad were actually counted, and "more than 70 percent of all absentee ballots reported not counted was because these ballots were returned to local election offices as undeliverable."

As a result, some Secretaries have spearheaded efforts to further facilitate the ability for those citizens to cast their ballots by examining methods for the transmission of a vote through the internet. In September 2008, five Secretaries of State traveled to Iraq to observe the election process from the perspective of citizens from their states serving in the military. Florida Secretary Browning, Indiana Secretary Rokita, Pennsylvania Secretary Cortés, Mississippi Secretary Hosemann, and California Secretary Bowen each traveled with representatives from the U.S. Department of Defense to speak to troops about voting procedures for overseas citizens and gather their views on how it can be improved. Following the trip, the first of its kind, Bowen developed a dedicated email address that

---

8 *Polling Place Accessibility Checklist*, California Secretary of State, March 2006, available at: http://www.sos.ca.gov/elections/corrected_final_ppasupplement_march17.pdf (accessed Aug. 22, 2009).

9 2006 Uniformed and Overseas Citizens Voting Act Survey, U.S. Elections Assistance Commission, Sept. 2007, http://www.eac.gov/News/docs/uocava-report-final-4-printing.pdf/attachment_download/file (accessed Aug. 22, 2009).

linked military and overseas voters to Bowen's staff for additional assistance, and a website with resources for military and overseas voters.[10]

Other Secretaries are developing innovative methods to ensure full access to the vote for voters living or serving abroad. Missouri Secretary Robin Carnahan provided voters from her state living overseas the option of faxing or emailing the ballots directly to local election officials at home. Similarly, in 2008 West Virginia Secretary Betty Ireland created a system to allow service personnel registered to vote in West Virginia to request and receive absentee ballots via email or fax, then either to fax or mail completed ballots back to the county clerks in the counties in which they are registered.[11] And Vermont Secretary Deb Markowitz works "within the context" of her state's laws to enable ballots to be "faxed or e-mailed overseas so that there can be a great chance of them being voted and then returned to Vermont by Election Day so that they can be counted." Markowitz also created a special page on her website for overseas and military voters "so that they can have easy access to all the information they need to register and vote by mail."

Amidst these innovations, in April 2008, Michael Dominguez, Principal Deputy Under Secretary of Defense for Personnel and Readiness, testified before a House Administration Committee that enabling electronic voting for service members may be the only solution available to address the difficulty of voting by mail that voters living overseas experience.[12] At that same congressional hearing, Alabama Secretary Beth Chapman, a champion for the cause of internet voting for voters enlisted in the military, said she shares some of the same concerns about security as Lungren, but concurred with Dominguez that internet voting is the only solution for ensuring access to the vote for these citizens. "With computer technology achieving feats that were once unimaginable," Chapman testified, "the problem of not allowing our military men and women every possible opportunity to vote is a travesty of justice."

Back home in Alabama, Chapman spent 2008 working incessantly to promote the passage of legislation to enable internet voting for those serving in the military from her state. To Chapman the barriers are "a huge travesty of justice" particularly because they affect "the very men and women who are fighting" to preserve democracy in other countries. And though UOCAVA "certainly allows them to vote absentee ballot, the timing is just not appropriate. Let's say there was an election regarding increased taxes that was not in the four year cycle,"

10 *Military and Overseas Voter Information*, California Secretary of State, available at: http://www.sos.ca.gov/elections/elections_mov.htm (accessed Aug. 22, 2009).

11 In previous elections, West Virginians living abroad could use only the mail system to receive and cast their absentee ballots. Rick Steelhammer, *W. Va. Military to Have E-mail, Fax Voting Option*, The Charleston Gazette, Aug. 27, 2008, available at: http://sundaygazettemail.com/News/200808260716.

12 Uniformed and Overseas Citizens Absentee Voting Act: Hearing Before the H. Comm. on House Administration, 110th Cong. 85 (2008) (statement of Michael Dominguez, Principal Deputy Under Secretary of Defense for Personnel and Readiness).

Chapman explains, "there's no way they would even have time to vote. And those are monumental decisions that will affect their lives. And they come home to whatever decision the rest of us made."

Frustrated with the lack of support for enabling online voting from the Alabama legislature, Chapman formed a military vote task force that brought vendors to meet with state legislators to demonstrate how internet voting works for military and overseas voters. The task force was specifically charged with "developing a plan of action for the implementation of a secure system for Internet voting for deployed military personnel and citizens of the state who are living overseas at election time." To Chapman,

> "it's really not a partisan issue because anybody who enlists in the military should [be able to vote just like anyone else]. I care that they're Americans and I care that they're willing to sacrifice their life for me, my family, and my entire country. [And] as far as having one of the highest if not the highest per capita percentages of men and women serving in the United States military, Alabama has got to get the legislation passed."

Alabama's neighbors in Florida have had more success in promoting this avenue of access to the ballot box. A local election official in Florida spearheaded "Operation Bravo," a pilot project that placed kiosks with computer stations on military bases in Germany, England, and Japan. During a ten-day period just before Election Day, some Florida voters living in those areas were able to enter a computer kiosk and vote on an encrypted electronic ballot, which was transmitted via a secure computer line to a data center in Spain, then to Florida. In addition, voters saw a printout of the ballots they cast prior to transmittal, and only Florida voting officials were able to view the encrypted information.[13]

Several voting rights activists resisted the reform, raising concerns that the ballots could be subject to tampering.[14] Representatives of the "Florida Voters Coalition" sent a letter to Secretary Browning outlining their concerns about the security of the ballots.[15] But Browning's staff worked diligently to review the source codes and test the reliability of the ballots, and the voting system was subsequently approved as secure by the Elections Assistance Commission in May 2009. Browning's Director of Elections Donald Palmer recalled that "there had never been a certification effort like this before and no federal guidelines upon which to base a testing regime; we were pioneers in this field."

---

13 Catherine Dolinski, *Activists Target Internet Voting*, Tampa Tribune, May 30, 2008, available at: http://www2.tbo.com/content/2008/may/30/me-internet-voting-targeted/.

14 Denver Post Wire Services, *Internet Voting Push Has Critics*, May 28, 2008, available at: http://origin.currentargus.com/ci_9397390.

15 The full text of the letter is available at: http://www.floridavoters.org/downloads/BrowningLetter052908.pdf (accessed Aug. 22, 2009).

To Secretary Chapman, this pioneering element can lead to resistance bases upon the "fear of the unknown." But Chapman says, "I've seen it done, I have seen examples, I have seen demonstrations. [Florida is] proving that it can work." And while security issues are "everyone's concern," Chapman notes that "the United States military created the internet, I think we can trust them to use it. If the men and women serving their country can't come to the polling place then we've got to take the polling place to them."

Conclusion

Whether reaching out to voters with disabilities, limited English proficiency, or those living or serving overseas, multiple Secretaries have worked to recognize that some communities of voters require additional accommodation and consideration to ensure their full access to the political process. As a result, several have gone above and beyond any relevant federal mandates to develop creative ways to ensure that all voters in their state enjoy clear avenues of access to the political process. And in developing and implementing these innovative accommodations, Secretaries not only embrace policies that facilitate greater voter participation, they send a message of inclusion to communities who may have faced conscious exclusion in the past.

It is also important to emphasize, however, that some of the most effective policies that Secretaries have independently developed have emerged through the involvement of and collaboration with members of the affected community in the decision-making process. In Maine, for example, Secretary Dunlap's announcement of a new voting system for disabled citizens included his emphasis that "many individuals" participated in the decision-making process, providing "invaluable" information, insights, and feedback. And for Florida Secretary Browning, traveling to Iraq enabled him, according to his state director of elections Donald Palmer, to view firsthand the barriers facing citizens serving in the military and "personally ask what the challenges … were and how they could be remedied."[16] And, Palmer noted in testimony to Congress, the "overwhelming response" from soldiers was their desire to have "the ability to vote via email." The soldiers also emphasized to Browning their anxiety and frustration over having to send in their ballots, "due to the fact that they are often not aware of the status of their ballot and whether they will receive it or whether it will be received back in the U.S. in time for counting." Browning was able to use this information to help support local efforts to enable electronic voting abroad.

The lesson, then, is not only that voters are better off when Secretaries proactively go above and beyond any federal requirements to ensure pathways to

---

16 Congressional testimony by the Director of Florida's Dept. of State Don Palmer, Senate Rules and Administration, Military and Overseas Voters, 2009 WLNR 9115517 (May 13, 2009).

the vote are clear for citizens facing unique barriers to casting their ballot. It is also that Secretaries must embrace the challenge of developing policies that promote access and participation, and ensure that members of the uniquely situated voting communities are actively involved in the process of developing solutions. In working collaboratively to develop solutions to barriers to voting, Secretaries can best ensure that the policies they implement are going to minimize those barriers and reflect the will of the community members. For those citizens are, in the words of Pennsylvania Secretary Pedro Cortés, not only the "experts in the field" but the "ultimate beneficiaries" of the results.

California Secretary of State Debra Bowen

First Elected: 2006

Few things are as vital to Debra Bowen as protecting the integrity of the electoral process. Shortly after taking office in California in 2006, she developed a team to implement a "Top to Bottom Review" of the state's electronic voting machines. When it became clear from the review that the machines could be manipulated to deliver false vote totals, Bowen decertified them all until they were able to meet with new additional standards for security.

"I think that there were a lot of people who were skeptical about certain election equipment," she recalled, "and I felt it was critical to do a top to bottom review of all voting systems used in California." The results led to widespread changes. In addition to finding "physical and technological security issues in the equipment," the group "found challenges like the legs of the stand that holds the voting equipment were too close together to allow a person in a wheelchair to use the machine." Under Bowen's leadership, the group decertified all electronic machines and instituted "a blueprint for voting equipment vendors to improve their goods."

Bowen's work has gone beyond the strides her leadership took in promoting better election technology. In the wake of controversies around biased election administration in other states, she has also sought to use her position affirmatively to promote the importance of impartial elections officials. "The reform that I would like to see," she noted, "would be something to prevent a Secretary of State from taking a position in a contest in which he or she is certifying the outcomes." It's a code of ethics, Bowen said, and a position that she has "voluntarily adopted." And it's a commitment that isn't without its difficulties. "People who you've known a long time and who helped you get elected will say 'Well, I support you, can you support me?'" she cautioned. "But my answer is always no, I can't. I don't want bias or even the appearance of bias. And were I to start endorsing or campaigning for candidates and there were a difficult call to be made about election procedures, people would have a right to be skeptical about my motivation."

Chapter 8
The Secretary as Voter Protector

"My role is to protect the voter and stand up for the rights of the voter. And that is not a partisan task."

Maine Secretary of State Matt Dunlap

A paramount and often unspoken duty of a state's chief elections official is to protect the integrity and accuracy of an election by ensuring that no voter is wrongfully blocked from voting on Election Day. This is particularly crucial because, in states where Secretaries oversee elections, they are typically the only entity with the defined responsibility of working to ensure that votes are cast and counted. As a result, the Secretary is often the primary statewide official to whom a voter can turn who will be able to prioritize the protection of their right to vote. They are, in a sense, the state's chief voter protector.

In recent years, Secretaries have developed a variety of approaches when they have embraced their responsibility to protect voters' rights. Some have developed comprehensive and proactive strategies, such as Ohio Secretary Brunner's Voting Rights Institute. The Institute's mission is to collect and address voters' concerns as they arise, while also proactively advocating for any changes to statutes or other policies that will address voters' concerns.

Other efforts have taken the form of periodic, intermittent policies that respond to potential immediate threats of voter harassment or erroneous challenges to a voter's eligibility. In September 2008, for example, Brunner issued a directive indicating that it was illegal to challenge a voter's eligibility if they were facing foreclosure, after rumors emerged that voters might face such challenges on Election Day 2008. And in the weeks leading up to the 2006 election, Michigan Secretary Terri Lynn Land issued a directive blocking challengers from speaking directly to voters inside the polling place.

Secretaries could also engage in efforts to protect the sanctity of what is placed on the ballot itself, such as programs to ensure individuals gathering signatures to place something on the ballot are not deceiving voters when soliciting their signatures. In Oregon, for example, anyone circulating ballot initiative petitions must apply for a license through the Secretary of State's office. Obtaining the license involves participating in a statewide training on the legalities of the signature collection process. If people collecting signatures don't comply with state election laws, or if they seek to collect signatures through fraud and misrepresentation, they risk losing their license to collect signatures.

In Kentucky, Secretary Trey Grayson responded quickly with a warning to citizens in his state in April 2008, upon learning that a nonpartisan organization had sent "thousands of potentially confusing mailings to women across Kentucky asking them to register to vote" after the deadline for the May primary had passed.[1] After receiving a letter from the head of the organization admitting that their mailings may cause voters to be confused about whether they were indeed registered to vote, Grayson held a press conference to remind voters of registration deadlines and encouraging them to check their voter registration at his official website. And that same month in Arizona, Secretary Jan Brewer admonished elections officials who were allegedly allowing representatives of the Democratic and Republican parties to obtain ballots for "independent testing"—allowing for the reproduction of ballots and compromising the integrity of the process.[2]

But by far the most prominent acts that Secretaries have taken in recent years to protect citizens' votes has involved their work to preserve the sanctity and accurate count of the ballots cast. As technology and funding has flowed to states seeking to upgrade or streamline their voting systems in recent years, many Secretaries have taken an active role in protecting the vote through ensuring that the methods and technology used in counting ballots are pure and untainted.

The Secretary and Counting the Vote

The role of the Secretary of State in selecting and implementing ballot counting technology has received increased attention in the post-2000 election world. This is due in part to the difficulties that emerged in Florida and Ohio in 2000 and 2004, and also due to the enactment of the Help America Vote Act (HAVA), which provided over $300 million for states wishing to replace outdated voting equipment, and $3 billion for other voting system improvements.[3] HAVA requires that any states receiving federal funds through the legislation maintain voting systems that meet certain standards, including providing the voter with the opportunity to correct any errors in their ballot before it is cast.[4] HAVA also requires that new machines have the capacity for audits and at least one in each polling place is accessible for individuals with disabilities.

Despite this federal support for improved technology, a 2007 report from Electionline.org and the Pew Center for the States reported that in many places, the new machines "have not instilled … confidence in the election systems."[5]

1 http://sos.ky.gov/secdesk/mediacenter/pressreleases/article166.htm (accessed June 20, 2009).

2 Andrea Kelly, *County Accused of Ballot Breach*, Arizona Daily Star, March 18, 2008, available at: http://www.azstarnet.com/metro/230176 (accessed June 12, 2009).

3 42 U.S.C.S. § 15481 (2002).

4 *Id.*

5 *The Help America Vote Act at 5*, ElectionLine.Org, Nov. 29, 2007, available at: http://www.pewcenteronthestates.org/uploadedFiles/HAVA.At.5.pdf (noting also that "[e]lectronic voting system glitches, snafus and full-blown breakdowns in Sarasota County,

To a certain extent, their research indicated that the actions of the Secretary of State were particularly important to ensuring that the transition to new machines promoted the dual goals of accuracy and access that the HAVA drafters sought to accomplish with the legal changes. When detailing some of the problems with the 2002 transition to new systems, the analysis specifically pointed to "poor training and machine glitches" as a "large part" of the "meltdown" that occurred in places such as Broward and Miami-Dade counties in Florida.[6] The authors noted, however, that the actions of a Secretary of State in nearby Georgia enabled a "far smoother transition to the new technology," particularly due to then-Secretary Cox's work to coordinate "detailed hands-on training and preparation" for all poll workers in the state.[7] But sometimes even heightened scrutiny and oversight of election poll workers is not enough. Secretary Bowen reasons, "California has almost 100,000 poll workers on election day, so somewhere someone is going to do something that's not in the instruction set. And so our question is: What will happen? Will we lose votes? Will we lose the count?"

Secretaries also have significant discretion over how to allocate or distribute machines in various precincts. In states that do not have specific legal requirements for how many machines the state must provide per voter, Secretaries can have a great deal of control over where to provide funding for additional machines.

During the 2004 presidential election, for example, then-Ohio Secretary Ken Blackwell was accused of not allocating enough machines in several locations, leading to voters having to wait in line in some precincts for as long as five hours.[8] During the day of the election, the Ohio Democratic Party filed suit against Blackwell on behalf of voters in two Ohio counties that did not have enough voting machines to accommodate the large numbers of citizens voting that day.[9] The lawsuit requested that the court order the boards of elections in both counties to provide other options for voters—namely, paper ballots—to use instead of waiting in line for hours to cast their vote.[10] A federal judge later that day mandated that paper ballots be provided to those still in line waiting to vote in the counties. The judge's order, however, did not—and indeed, could not—provide a complete remedy for many of the voters who still waited in line for several hours after the polls had closed in order to cast their vote.[11]

Fla., Carteret County, N.C., Montgomery County, Md. and other localities have eroded confidence in paperless systems").

6 *Id.*

7 *Id.* (citing *Election Reform Since 2001: What's Changed, What Hasn't and Why*, electionline.org, Oct. 2002).

8 Daniel P. Tokaji, *Law and Democracy: A Symposium on the Law Governing Our Democratic Process*, 73 Geo. Wash. L. Rev. 1206 at 1238 (2005); See also *id.* at 1220–22: (detailing the causes and results of Ohio's failure to upgrade all of their voting machines by 2004).

9 *Id.* at 1238.

10 *Id.*

11 *Id.* at 1239.

A third area of development in election technology involves questions regarding the accuracy and reliability of voting systems. At the center of much of the controversy are Direct Recording Electronic (DREs) machines, which many critics argue are subject to tampering and other security concerns.[12] Across the country, Secretaries of State have led the charge to investigate the concerns. In 2007 alone, chief state election officials in Colorado, Kentucky, Ohio, and California engaged in systematic investigations into the reliability and accuracy of their voting systems. When those concerns are credible, they have decertified machines or worked to provide other options for voting that prove secure, accurate, or reliable.

Long before the Secretaries in those states began their investigations, New Hampshire Secretary Bill Gardner was speaking out about his concerns about the security of electronic voting systems. In 1986, his state banned punch card voting machines, the same machines that were the source of so many problems in the Florida 2000 election. Indeed, "Florida," Gardner recalled, "was a déjà vu for us because the same things that happened there had happened" in New Hampshire in the 1980s.

And like Florida, after punch card machines were banned in 1986, one New Hampshire community—Manchester—selected electronic voting machines (DREs) as a replacement. Gardner recalls that at the time "a computer [scientist] went to the local officials" to warn them about the problems of electronic voting. "You shouldn't use these machines," Gardner recalled him saying to the local officials in Manchester at the time. But the officials ignored the expert's warnings and purchased the machines anyway. And in the second election to use the machines, there was a close election for mayor in which the two candidates were separated by a small margin. "And when it came time for the recount," Gardner recalled,

> "instead of doing it the way I always do it, with the paper ballots, [we] just pushed a button [to view the results]. And the loser said 'Is that all there is?' And then the winner said 'I agree, this isn't right.' And so two [state legislators] from Manchester put a bill in that required that from that point on, everyone in New Hampshire had to vote on a paper ballot."

Two decades later, California Secretary of State Debra Bowen took the oath of office in her state with an eye towards initiating a full review of the state's electronic voting machines. Bowen was bolstered by a statutory mandate that required her to periodically review voting systems to see if they are defective, obsolete, or otherwise unacceptable. "I think that there were a lot of people who

12 See, e.g., Tim Padgett, *Voting Out E-Voting Machines*, Time Magazine, Nov. 3, 2007, available at: http://www.time.com/time/nation/article/0,8599,1680451,00.html; see also Jim McElhatton, *Touch Screen Voting Faulted*, Wash. Times, Feb. 18, 2004, at B01 (describing concerns with the security of electronic voting systems).

were skeptical about certain election equipment," she recalled, "and I had made a pledge, a campaign pledge, to do a top to bottom review of all voting systems."

To complete the "top to bottom review," Bowen enlisted a team of renowned computer scientists to administer this review of the California electronic voting machines. Bowen recalls: "I had the advantage of having a contract with the University of California to undertake the review fairly rapidly, which turned out to be very important. I didn't have much time."

The team evaluated the security of three types of voting machines from three different manufacturers: Diebold Elections Systems, Sequoia Voting Systems and Hart InterCivic. And when the report was finished, Bowen was faced with an unanticipated decision. "Some of what we focused on I think we expected to find," she remembers. "We knew that we were going to find physical and technological security issues in the equipment." But the team's research revealed that it was possible that an individual would be able to introduce viruses into a single machine that could manipulate vote tallies and then spread to other machines throughout the California voting system.[13] The report found that the system errors were found across the board on all three machines, and cited specific evidence that the "Diebold software contains vulnerabilities that could allow an attacker to install malicious software …, which could cause votes to be recorded incorrectly or to be miscounted, possibly altering election results."[14]

Upon reviewing the report, Bowen announced that she was decertifying the three electronic voting systems pending further review: "basically we created a blueprint for voting equipment vendors to improve their goods." The "blueprint" enabled the recertification of machines once it could be shown that they met the security measures laid out in the "blueprint." Essentially, Bowen described, her decision "was a withdrawal of approval and an immediate reapproval [of the machines] with additional conditions. All of the systems that we looked at had additional conditions imposed."

Shortly thereafter, Colorado Secretary of State Mike Coffman followed suit, decertifying almost all of the electronic voting machines used in his state and instituting "stringent testing requirements for electronic voting machines."[15] Ohio came next.

---

13 Nicole Winger, *California Secretary of State Debra Bowen Comments on Field Poll About Voter Confidence in Elections*, US Fed News Service, Aug. 23, 2007.

14 For the full text of the decertification order, see *Withdrawal of Approval of Diebold Elections Systems*, California Secretary of State, available at: http://www.sos.ca.gov/elections/voting_systems/ttbr/diebold_102507.pdf (accessed June 12, 2009).

15 The new testing procedures were adopted under the Secretary's rulemaking authority and were dubbed "Rule 45." The Rule included forty-six pages of requirements for voting systems certification, including detailed security standards for all voting systems. The new certification process involved 437 functional tests that a voting system will need to pass in order to be certified for use in Colorado. For more information, see: *Coffman Strengthens Testing Requirements for Electronic Voting Machines*, March 20, 2007, available at: http://www.sos.state.co.us/pubs/rule_making/rule_45_adoption_final.pdf (accessed June 12, 2009).

In late 2007, reacting to complaints arising out of the 2004 election, Ohio Secretary Jennifer Brunner assembled a team of highly qualified computer scientists to evaluate the machines and test their reliability. Their study was dubbed the "Everest Report," an acronym for the "Evaluation and Validation of Election-Related Equipment, Standards and Testing." The research was spearheaded by two separate teams of scientists who conducted parallel assessments of the security of two of the three voting systems at the heart of the California study: Hart InterCivic and Premier Election Solutions (formerly Diebold), along with Election Systems & Software (ES&S). In addition, a bipartisan team of twelve local election officials served as advisors to the study. They evaluated all of the reports, and worked with Brunner to develop recommendations for changes.

Brunner's report not only revealed that the machines were potentially vulnerable to computer viruses and other sophisticated manipulations,[16] they also found that "fairly simple techniques" could alter the reliability of the machines. In announcing the report, Brunner noted that "in every-day terms, the tools needed to compromise an accurate vote count could be as simple as tampering with the paper audit trail connector or using a magnet and a personal digital assistant."[17]

Because under Ohio law voting machines are chosen at the local level, Brunner was unable to issue a sweeping decertification of all electronic voting machines throughout the state without the backing of the state legislature. But as a result of the EVEREST report's findings, Brunner was still able to issue several directives and push the state legislature to order the elimination of Ohio's electronic voting machines. Brunner's most significant directive required that all voters throughout the state be offered the option of voting via optical scan machines. She recalls:

> "I wanted to get the state on a completely paper ballot system, but the legislature wasn't willing to do it, [and] the state budget made it difficult. So, with the back-up paper ballots, which were tested in the primary, we at least could provide anyone who wanted a paper ballot to get one whenever and wherever they voted. And while that made it a little more cumbersome for the board in processing in the end, it still took care of the voters first and put [their] interest first."

Beyond protecting the integrity of the elections through increased oversight and scrutiny of the machines and ballot counting technology, many Secretaries have included an additional check: random audits. After Bowen decertified the majority of electronic voting machines in California, some computer science professors in her state issued additional warnings that the optical scan machines she'd replaced them with could be "prone to an equal amount of error because

---

16 The full report, published December 14, 2007, can be found at: http://www.sos.state.oh.us/sos/upload/everest/00-SecretarysEVERESTExecutiveReport.pdf.

17 *Study: Voting Systems Vulnerable*, Ohio Secretary of State, http://www.sos.state.oh.us/SOS/elections/voterInformation/equipment/VotingSystemReviewFindings.aspx (accessed June 30, 2009).

the machine cannot read marks which are recorded too lightly and may mistake stray marks as votes cast."[18]

California Elections Code § 15360 required elections officials conduct a manual count of 1 percent of the precincts in the election chosen at random. But Bowen instituted another rule that requires a hand audit of 10 percent of all ballots cast in closer races.[19] The Post-Election Manual Tally (PEMT) Regulations require an additional audit when a contest has a margin of victory of less than one half of one percent (0.5%), based on the semi-official final election results that traditionally come out on election night. "The goal here is accuracy," Bowen explained at the time, "and giving people confidence that the result is accurate."[20]

Bowen developed the rule in consultation with an audit working group she created to examine best practices of hand counting and auditing the vote in other states. "The working group was small," she recalled,

> "because we had a very limited time frame. It was small, five or six people, a county registrar, the executive director of the California voter foundation, a longtime nonpartisan advocate for voters' rights, a CPA, [and] a statistician. [W]e tried to cover the spectrum and asked them to do just sort of basic homework so that we could start the process. I expect that we'll be revising and refining as we go through election cycles."

In Connecticut, Secretary Susan Bysiewicz enforces one of the most extensive audit requirements in the country. Connecticut law specifically requires that local registrars conduct a manual audit in at least 10 percent of the voting districts in their jurisdiction.[21] In 2006, Bysiewicz partnered with computer scientists from the University of Connecticut Voting Technology Research Center (VoTeR) to review the security and reliability of her state's voting equipment. Although VoTeR does not assist in the collection of the post-election audit data, the Secretary of State uses

18 Neha Jaganathan, *Paper Ballots Return to Voting System*, The Daily Bruin, Jan. 31, 2008, available at: http://www.dailybruin.ucla.edu/news/2008/jan/31/paper-ballots-return-voting-system/.

19 The initial sample size for PEMT audits is 10 percent for local contests involving fewer than 100 precincts, 5 percent for state contests and local contests involving more than 100 precincts, and 2 percent for statewide contests. The regulations require additional precincts to be counted by hand if the audit uncovers significant variances between the manual tally and the machine tally. If significant variances persist, the regulations require all votes in the contest to be counted by hand to verify the election results.

20 Tim Moran, *California Secretary of State Aims to Fine-tune How We Vote*, Modesto Bee, June 27, 2008, available at: http://www.modbee.com/local/story/341979.html.

21 Public Act No. 07-1947 (1)(a) ("Not earlier than the fifteenth day after any election or primary and not later than two business days before the canvass of votes … the registrars of voters shall conduct a manual audit of the votes recorded in not less than ten per cent of the voting districts in the state, district or municipality, whichever is applicable. Such manual audit shall be noticed in advance and be open to public observation").

VoTeR's analysis to perform additional information-gathering and investigation and, in some cases, conduct an independent hand count of the ballots.

"They conduct memory card audits before each election," she explained, in order to

> "confirm that cards are properly programmed and that there's been no tampering prior to the election. And then they conduct a post-election audit of memory cards to make sure that there's no hacking or fraud on Election Day. We've always had very secure elections, but I think now we've built a foundation for very secure elections into the future."

And in Georgia, Secretary Karen Handel similarly developed a partnership with an Election Center at Kennesaw State University. The Center provides "outside, independent testing of the equipment leading into each election." And, Handel noted, through the Center's research "we discovered really basic things. It simply had not been covered in poll worker training, for example, to be sure that security codes are indeed kept secure."

The Secretary and Voter Protection

Though Secretaries have varying authority to legally intervene and block acts of intimidation on Election Day, many work within the bounds of their office to institute polices to shield voters from harassment when they are in the act of casting their ballot. Such statewide instructions and regulations can guard against intimidation and disruption from "challengers," or representatives of political parties and other groups present in the polling place.[22]

In *From Registration to Recounts*, the Center for Election Law @ Moritz discusses the benefits of such protections, particularly their potential for "deterring voter fraud or other improper attempts to influence elections."[23] The Center's research led its authors to make a number of recommendations to ensure that the accuracy and integrity benefits of a challenger process are offset or accompanied with procedures to protect voters' access to the polls. Among their suggestions are the importance of a challenge procedure providing "adequate due process to

---

22 In an effort to limit the potential for intimidation and harassment, the Michigan Secretary of State, for example, has issued regulations that forbid challengers from speaking to voters in the polling place. See http://www.michigan.gov/documents/sos/ELNEWs56_219590_7.pdf (published Dec. 21, 2007) (declaring that "challengers do not have the authority to approach voters or talk to voters in the polls or within 100 feet of any doorway being used by voters to enter the building in which the polling place is located").

23 Steven F. Huefner, Daniel P. Tokaji, and Edward B. Foley, *From Registration to Recounts: The Election Ecosystems of Five Midwestern States*, A publication of Election Law @ Moritz 178 (2007).

voters, including an opportunity to present evidence demonstrating their eligibility to vote" and a process that "deter[s] an overly aggressive use of challenges."[24]

Recent events in Michigan illustrate how a challenge process can go awry and the impact that a Secretary of State can have in attempting to limit future problems. In a 1999 city election in Hamtramck, Michigan, members of a group named Citizens for a Better Hamtramck placed challengers, as permitted under state law in Michigan, in over half of the polling locations throughout the city.[25] Throughout the day, the organization's challengers questioned the eligibility of over forty voters with Arabic-sounding surnames.[26] Once "challenged," a CCBH member required the voter to take an oath of citizenship, in English, in order to vote,[27] even if the challenged voter was able to produce an American passport.[28] The U.S. Department of Justice subsequently sued the city of Hamtramck for approving the organization and allowing the challengers to treat the voters in a discriminatory fashion.[29]

Several years later, a few days before the November 2006 election, Michigan Secretary Terri Lynn Land issued a policy that banned the use of video cameras, cell phones, cameras, televisions, and recording equipment from the polls "to ensure that all voters … have a full opportunity to exercise their right to vote in private without undue distractions or discomfort."[30] The regulations also, for the first time, prohibited challengers from approaching or talking to voters "for any reason."[31]

---

24 *Id.*

25 See Jocelyn F. Benson, *¡Su Voto Es Su Voz! Incorporating Limited English Proficient Voters into American Democracy*, 48 B. C. L.REV. 251 at 298 (2007).

26 U.S. Complaint, *U.S. v. Hamtramck*, No. 0073541 (E.D. Mich. 2000) at 1 ("This action arises out of the general election that took place in Hamtramck, Michigan on November 2, 1999. In that election, more than forty dark skinned or Arab American citizens were required to take an oath as a condition to voting, a requirement that was not imposed on white voters").

27 *Id.*

28 Consent Decree, *U.S. v. Hamtramck*, No. 0073541 (E.D. Mich. 2000) at 4 ("Some voters were challenged before they signed their applications to vote, and therefore appear to have been challenged based on their physical appearance alone. Other voters were challenged after they had signed their applications and their names had been announced. The challenged voters had dark skin and distinctly Arabic names, such as Mohamed, Ahmed, and Ali. The challengers did not appear to possess or consult any papers or lists to determine who to challenge").

29 *Id.*

30 *News You Can Use*, Michigan Secretary of State, Sept. 8, 2006, available at: http://www.michigan.gov/documents/sos/Issue_40_177190_7.pdf (making exceptions for broadcast stations and news media representatives to be present in certain areas of the polling room. "Regardless of whether a film crew making such a request positions themselves in the public area of the polling place or the entryway to the polling room, the precinct chairperson must supervise the filming process to ensure that the secrecy of the ballot is fully protected and no voters are inconvenienced by the filming process").

31 *Id.*

While this broad ban itself led to some confusion on behalf of political parties wishing to place representatives at the polling locations on Election Day to assist voters in the voting process,[32] the Secretary's act protected voters from harmful acts of less innocent organizations such as Citizens for a Better Hamtramck.

Another example came out of Ohio in September 2008, when rumors emerged that individual "challengers" might be placed in the polls to question the eligibility of voters whose homes were in foreclosure. The reasoning was that voters whose voter registration address was a home that was in foreclosure may have already moved or relocated to a new residence. Thus, if they appeared to vote on Election Day, they potentially would be casting a vote as a resident of a home where they no longer lived.

State and federal protections ensure voters who have moved within a certain time period or geographical area are still able to vote one final time at their previous address. But some individuals, it was rumored at the time, were planning to be in the polls on Election Day, challenging any voter who showed up to vote from a residency that was in foreclosure. Brunner cut through much of this confusion, issuing a directive from her office indicating that a citizen voting from a residence in foreclosure could not be blocked from casting their ballot.[33]

"[B]oards of elections," Brunner's directive advised, "may not cancel an Ohioan's voter registration based solely on the fact that the person is involved in the foreclosure process." Brunner continued, "mere involvement in a foreclosure action does not, by definition, mean that an elector no longer resides at the address that is the subject of the foreclosure." Because a voter could "continue to reside at an address throughout the pendency of a foreclosure action," Brunner explained, "a foreclosure action is, on its own, insufficient to sustain a voter registration challenge."[34]

Conclusion

Whether protecting the results and integrity of elections, or instituting guidelines that physically protect voters at polling locations on Election Day, many Secretaries have taken their role as voter protector very seriously, and to far-reaching results. Bowen's initiative in reviewing and subsequently decertifying voting systems throughout the entire state of California, Land's policies to shield voters from

32 Amber Hunt and John Wisely, *Turnout High, with Some Glitches, Workers Say*, Detroit Free Press, Nov. 8, 2006, at 11 (describing lawsuits filed on Election Day in Detroit, Michigan over compliance with the Secretary of State's ban on challengers talking to voters).

33 Advisory, *Voting Rights of Persons Facing Home Foreclosure*, Sept. 24, 2008, available at: http://www.sos.state.oh.us/SOS/elections/Directives/2008%20Advisories/2008-25.aspx.

34 *Id.*

harassment on Election Day, and Brunner's efforts to ensure voters have the option of voting with a paper ballot all serve to underscore the significant effect the actions of a Secretary of State can have on promoting the accuracy and integrity of elections.

But in many ways, for Secretaries in states where they are charged with overseeing elections, this role as voter protector is a crucial responsibility. Various statewide entities can stake a claim to wanting to protect voters. The state Attorney General, for example, may have the authority to investigate and prosecute fraud in elections. But where they oversee the elections process, Secretaries are in a position unlike any other statewide entity to prioritize and focus on developing uniform systems to protect voters' rights. It is because of that unparalleled position that it is so crucial for Secretaries to advance policies and practices that protect both voters and the integrity of the election process.

Finally, there is a tangential impact on democracy when Secretaries serve as the state's chief protector of voting rights. In order to participate actively as voters, citizens must have confidence in the process itself. In fact, preserving and promoting voters' confidence in the process is fundamental to protecting democracy. When Secretaries are actively using their position to develop methods for protecting voters' rights, they restore and encourage voters' faith in the electoral system as a whole. Restoring and encouraging this faith leads to a more engaged citizenry and a healthier democratic process.

Ohio Secretary of State
Jennifer Brunner

First Elected: 2006

Prior to her election as Secretary of State, Jennifer Brunner had an illustrious career as an attorney, specializing in election law. Upon taking office in 2007, her first priority was to "make sure that we always protected the integrity of the vote." And "that was certainly easy to accomplish," she believes "while you are ensuring that voting was accessible, transparent, and easy to understand." For Brunner, making voting accessible and secure means a more engaged and educated citizenry. "If you can take away some of the difficulties of the mechanics of voting and concerns about security," she reasoned, "then you free people up to think more about the real issues and the candidates. You have a more informed citizenry, and so the voting process is resulting in the true expression of the will of the people."

In the months leading up to the 2008 presidential election, Brunner was keen to reform the voting process prior to one of the most pivotal elections in American history. She created a policy that ensured any voter in her state would have the option of voting with a paper ballot. "I wanted to get the state on a completely paper ballot system," she noted, "but the legislature wasn't willing to do it. So, with the back-up paper ballots, we at least could provide anyone who wanted a paper ballot to get one whenever and wherever they voted." As a result, though the reform "made it a little more cumbersome for the board in processing in the end, it still took care of the voters first and put the interest of the voters first."

For Brunner, who took office on the heels of Ohio becoming the poster child for poorly run elections under former Secretary Kenneth Blackwell, instituting these types of reforms were critical to restore voters' confidence in Ohio's elections. "I really love my state," she reflected, "and it really pained to see how we were portrayed, seeing how it damaged peoples' confidence in the process." Her reward came on election night 2008, "when they called Ohio, there was not a lawsuit, they kept the polls open late, and it was a smooth day." For Brunner, "when you can actually open up the process and bring people into the process, you see what good things come out of it. And that's what democracy is all about."

Chapter 9
The Secretary as Enforcer

> "There's a freedom fighter aspect to this. We are on the front lines of protecting an idea, and the idea is that the best way to run a society is when the people pick their own leaders. So as much as I want everyone to participate and try to encourage that, I get a lot of satisfaction in making sure that the process is defended."
>
> Indiana Secretary of State Todd Rokita

Nebraska Secretary John Gale knows that as his state's chief elections officer, he wears "several different hats." But in his view, his primary job as Secretary of State is to "ensure that the election laws of the state and federal governments are enforced." As a result, Gale keeps several attorneys on his staff and maintains "close contact with the 93 county attorneys and the county election officials to answer any and all questions they might have regarding the 220 pages of election laws and 700 provisions contained in those pages of election laws." To Gale, "enforcing the laws and ensuring that our election officials are trained and knowledgeable about the laws is certainly the top priority."

As the state's chief interpreter, administrator, and enforcer of election laws, the Secretary is charged with ensuring that mountainous volumes of state laws regulating elections are implemented accurately and evenly throughout the state. And one of the difficulties many Secretaries face is ensuring that their office has sufficient resources to enable them to enforce the laws.

To Oregon Secretary Bill Bradbury, one of the most surprising aspects of his job was the lack of resources his office had at their disposal to support the implementation and enforcement of the laws on the books. "We have wanted to have one or two paid investigators on staff to really look at some of the problems, particularly more in the [ballot] initiative area," Bradbury recalled.

> "And what really frustrated me was that nobody has yet succeeded in the legislature to fund an investigator or two for the Secretary of State. [And because] the role of the Secretary of State is fundamentally oversight of elections, a fundamental part of that should be to have some investigative ability as well. … I don't know where the resistance comes from for the funding in an investigator or two. That seems to me to be critical in being able to implement the laws fairly and effectively."

Secretaries also struggle to ensure the laws are followed at the local level and that, when violations occur, local officials are held accountable. Colorado Secretary Mike Coffman developed one of the most effective tools to achieving that end. He created an Election Watch List that listed counties that had experienced significant problems in conducting their elections. Aiming to promote voter confidence in elections where local officials had encountered problems in the past, Coffman would place any county on the list that violated certain legal requirements or was found to have mismanaged an election "to such an extent that it creates unreasonable obstacles for citizens attempting to vote." Counties placed on the list received a written "description of their deficiencies, as well as an outline of the corrective action necessary for removal from the list." Coffman's office worked closely with counties on the Watch List to address any remaining issues before the next election. And if a county or local official did not succeed in rectifying any of the problems, Coffman would seek a court order giving his office direct supervision over the conduct of the county's next election, which he was entitled to do under Colorado law. The list, Coffman emphasized at the time, was meant to promote collaboration between his office and local officials. "This policy is meant to be helpful, not punitive," he emphasized.[1]

Four counties were placed under the initial Watch List in March of 2007. Some were removed later that year. One was Denver, placed on the Watch List after voters in the city experienced excessive wait times during the 2006 election.[2] Denver was removed from the list in October 2008, after a newly elected clerk implemented changes to improve poll worker staffing and recruitment.

The Secretary Enforcing Voter Registration Requirements

Beyond the general enforcement of the law, most Secretaries of State serve as the principal keeper of the statewide voter file, which lists all of the registered voters in the state.[3] In those states, the Secretary is primarily responsible for maintaining, managing, or removing voters from voter registration lists. It is critical that, in furtherance of this authority, they work to maintain the accuracy of the data in the voter file.

Under federal law, both HAVA and the NVRA establish limitations for when officials can remove or "purge" voters from federal registration lists.[4] HAVA

---

1 See, *News Release: Coffman Announces "Election Watch List" Initiative*, Colorado Secretary of State, March 12, 2007, available at: http://www.sos.state.co.us/pubs/pressrel/election_watch_list_initiative.html (accessed July 28, 2009).

2 *News Release: Coffman Removes Denver from State's Watch List*, Colorado Secretary of State, Oct. 24, 2008, available at: http://www.sos.state.co.us/pubs/pressrel/denver_watch_list_removal_10-24-08.pdf (accessed July 28, 2009).

3 Under HAVA, each state accepting federal funds was required to develop and maintain a statewide voter file.

4 See, e.g., 42 U.S.C. 1973gg-6(a)(4). Though the NVRA applies only to protect voters who register to vote in federal elections, states typically maintain only one registration list, and consider voters who register and vote in federal elections to be duly registered for state and local elections. Thus the requirements that are applicable for federal registration lists implicitly apply to all state held voter registration lists.

Section 303(a) requires that states periodically remove voters who are registered twice, have moved, died, or otherwise are ineligible. The NVRA mandates that state authorities periodically make a "reasonable effort to remove the names of ineligible voters" from the list of registered voters if they die, move, or otherwise become ineligible to vote where they are registered. The Act also includes a provision, however, that prohibits the removal of inactive voters until they have failed to vote in two consecutive federal elections. In addition, the NVRA requires that election officials complete any list maintenance, and remove any ineligible voters, no later than ninety days before a federal election.[5]

A primary purpose behind both federal requirements is to ensure that any state effort to remove voters from registration lists is done in a fair, uniform, and nondiscriminatory manner that does not diminish the participation of any eligible voters. But both statutes lack specific guidelines or instructions to states as to how to remove ineligible voters from their lists. As a result, voter eligibility and purge decisions are left almost completely to state and local election officials.

The New York Times picked up on some of the problems with this in 2004. "If [local] election offices had adequate resources and precise rules," the paper wrote, "voting lists might accurately reflect who is entitled to vote. But the reality is far more chaotic, and errors abound."[6] For example, one 2004 report on registration list management surveyed maintenance policies in fifteen states. The study found that none of the states surveyed required its election officials to use "any specific or minimum criteria to ensure that an individual with a felony conviction is the same individual being purged from the voter rolls." Two-thirds of the states did not even require election officials to notify voters that they had been removed from the registration lists. The DEMOS report concluded that "states, even those with identical disfranchisement policies, conduct purges very unevenly because of flawed or nonexistent legislative guidance. As a result, legal voters, including voters who share similar names with felons, are mistakenly taken off of voter rolls."[7]

State Secretaries of State can play a significant role in working with local officials to promote better list management. In November 2005, the United States Justice Department sued Secretary Carnahan under the NVRA, claiming she'd violated the law's requirement to "conduct a general program that makes a reasonable effort to remove the names of ineligible voters from the official lists

---

5 *Id.* States may only remove voters from the registration list closer than ninety days before an election if they are reported dead, mentally incompetent to vote, or become ineligible under any felon disenfranchisement law.

6 Editorial, *How America Doesn't Vote*, New York Times, Feb. 15, 2004.

7 Laleh Ispahani, *Purged! How a Patchwork of Flawed and Inconsistent Voting Systems Could Deprive Millions of Americans of the Right to Vote*, A Publication of the American Civil Liberties Union and DEMOS, Oct. 19, 2004, available at: http:ww/aclu.org/FilesPDFs/purged-voting-report.pdf (accessed July 28, 2009).

of eligible voters" by reason of death or change in residency.[8] In July 2008 the Eighth U.S. Circuit Court of Appeals concluded that Carnahan had the ultimate responsibility for enforcing the law and ensuring the registration lists were accurate and up to date by doing everything she could to promote compliance on the local level. The court held that while Carnahan "cannot be required to enforce the act against [local election authorities], any lack of [local] compliance remains relevant to determining whether or not Missouri is reasonably conducting a general program."[9] The Eighth Circuit instructed the lower court to review Carnahan's efforts, which included training local officials on list maintenance, and assess whether she was doing everything she could to promote list accuracy.

At the same time, in 2003 the actions of then-Florida Secretary Katherine Harris illustrated how errors or missteps of the state's chief election official can result in an elimination of access to the electoral process. In the months following the November 2000 presidential election, information came to light through a series of investigations that Harris had hired a private firm to compile a list of registered voters who were ineligible to vote under Florida's restrictive felon disenfranchisement law.[10]

The United States Commission on Civil Rights conducted hearings after the election to investigate the actions of the firm. Evidence presented at these hearings revealed Secretary Harris had dismissed the advice of the private firm and removed the names of thousands of voters whose names barely matched the names of individuals convicted of felonies.[11] In addition, many of the voters wrongly removed by Harris's purge were African Americans, who in Florida are also strong Democratic voters. This prompted many individuals to question whether there were partisan motives behind the purge.[12]

---

8 National Voter Registration Act of 1993, 42 U.S.C. 1973gg-6(a)(4).

9 *United States v. Missouri*, 535 F.3d 844, 851 (8th Cir. 2008).

10 Florida's election code denies individuals from voting for life if they are convicted in any state of any felon. See Fla. Const. art. VI, § 4. It is possible for voting rights to be restored after application to a state executive review board, though in practice only a few clemencies have been granted. See, e.g., Jason Grotto and Debbie Cenziper, *Clemency System Veiled in Secrecy*, Miami Herald, Nov. 14, 2004 at 16A.

11 See, Robert E. Pierre, *Botched Name Purge Denied Some the Right to Vote*, Wash. Post, May 31, 2001 at A01, available at: http://www.washingtonpost.com/ac2/wp-dyn/A99749-2001May30 (describing one woman who was removed because her sister had been convicted of a felony and was ineligible to vote).

12 See Editorial, *supra* note 6; see also, Richard L. Hasen, *Beyond the Margin of Litigation: Reforming U.S. Election Administration to Avoid Electoral Meltdown*, 62 Wash. & Lee L. Rev. 937, 965–66 (noting that the Harris list of voters to purge from the list "included a number of 'false positives,' that is, persons who should not have been listed as felons. The error in part was caused by the name-matching program used by the private company, in which nonfelons with names similar to felons were placed on the purge list. It appears that somewhere between 1,000 and 8,000 eligible voters—many African-

In 2004, the Florida Department of State, under the leadership of a new Secretary of State, hired a different private firm to develop a system for removing ineligible voters, particularly convicted felons, from the registration list. But unlike the state voter registration list, the state's criminal records did not include information as to which individuals were of Hispanic descent. As a result of these two incompatible databases, "approximately 22,000 African American voters were scheduled to be purged from the official Florida voter database, while just slightly more than 60 Hispanic voters were tagged for removal."[13] After public interest groups loudly voiced their concerns about her actions, the Secretary of State cancelled the purge.

It is important that any effort to keep voter registration rolls "current" through the periodic removal of ineligible voters includes a safety net to make sure that any purging errors do not result in the removal of an otherwise eligible voter. In 2006, Kentucky Secretary of State Trey Grayson announced a program to clean the registration rolls by removing 8,105 Kentucky voters who had more recently registered in Tennessee or South Carolina. Almost 200 of those voters appeared to vote in the election immediately following the removal. But under the program, no voters were turned away because they were still allowed to cast their ballot if they could provide proof that they still lived in Kentucky.

It is also important to ensure that any voters in danger of being removed from the rolls are notified beforehand, to ensure that voter participation is not wrongfully minimized through any purging efforts. Notification is important in promoting access because it enables voters to address any errors and to ensure they are able to vote if they are legally eligible. For example, while Virginia law does not require election officials to provide notice to voters who are removed from the registration list under the state's felon disenfranchisement law, the Virginia Board of Elections encourages local elections officials to send a notice of cancellation to such voters, along with information on how to challenge the removal or restore their voting rights. Such a practice exemplifies how a state's chief election authority can independently ensure that while accuracy and integrity are promoted through the removal of ineligible voters from registration lists, voter rights and access to participation are not wrongly affected through the removal of otherwise eligible citizens.[14]

Americans with Democratic voter registrations—were removed from the list because they were incorrectly identified as ineligible former Florida felons").

13 Chris Davis and Matthew Doig, *Voter Purge Decision Could Haunt Jeb Bush*, Sarasota Herald-Trib., July 13, 2004 ("No one at the division of elections … recognized that Hispanics were almost non-existent on the list, which contained 24,197 whites and 22,084 blacks. Hispanics made up 61 names on the list, though they represent 17% of the state's population").

14 In 2006, the Secretary of State in Kentucky came under fire from the state Attorney General after he did not notify voters who were removed from Kentucky's list because of a potential change in residency. See: *Attorney General Stumbo Challenges State Board of Elections and Secretary of State on Number of Eligible Voters Purged*, Sept. 18, 2006, http://www.kentucky.gov/Newsroom/aag/eligiblevoterspurged.htm (accessed July 28, 2009).

The Secretary Enforcing Laws Against Fraud in Elections

Beyond enforcing the accuracy and maintenance of lists, several Secretaries have taken steps to ensure that false names are not entered into the file to begin with. In Washington in 2006, Secretary Sam Reed heard reports from local elections officials who had found that a nonprofit organization had submitted over 1,700 "blatantly fraudulent voter registrations" with "forged names." In early 2007, Reed "got the prosecutor in King County to really go after" the organization. Reed saw to it that the prosecutors "tracked these people down all the way to Baltimore and got confessions from all seven of them. And their confession was that they went to the Seattle public library and pulled out phone books and just started writing down names and then they would just switch them around and different ones would sign" the forms. Eventually, felony charges were filed against seven individuals and the organization was fined $25,000.[15]

In serving as the catalyst for the investigation and subsequent prosecution of the offenders, Reed experienced firsthand how crucial it is for the state's chief elections official to enforce the law. Reed shouldered a great deal of the burden in ensuring the investigation moved forward because the prosecutors "have priorities, and they tend to be short staffed. And so something like a voter registration problem is the least of their worries. So, yes it was very important that I really pushed them hard. And we did [make statements to] the press that we will not tolerate voter [registration] fraud in our state."

Alabama Secretary Beth Chapman cites fighting fraudulent behavior as one of her priorities in ensuring "fair and honest elections." She created a Voter Fraud unit, headed by a former Justice on the Alabama Supreme Court with a background in prosecuting cases of voter fraud prior to his tenure on the bench. The unit established a "Stop Voter Fraud Now" website and a hotline for individuals to report any allegations of fraud that merit further investigation. Any complaints received are forwarded directly to the Attorney General's office or prosecutor's office. In Chapman's view, housing a unit of that sort in her office encouraged citizens who may be intimidated by the thought of reporting allegations to the Alabama Attorney General would be more "comfortable" reporting such claims to her office. And though Chapman's office does not investigate the complaint, she feels that the creation of the department "seems to have deterred a lot of people from attempting voter fraud, which is really good news for us."

Other Secretaries have developed new and innovative strategies for enforcing election law. Chapman's neighbor in Georgia, Secretary Karen Handel, also created a separate investigative unit in her office that employs several dozen individuals "with law enforcement and investigative backgrounds." On Election Day, the

15 Keith Ervin, *Felony Charges Filed Against 7 in State's Biggest Case of Voter Registration Fraud*, The Seattle Times, July 26, 2007, available at: http://seattletimes.nwsource.com/html/localnews/2003806904_webvotefraud26m.html (accessed July 28, 2009).

investigators serve as monitors all around the state. With representatives from her office on the ground, in place throughout the state, Handel is able to respond quickly to any issues at the precinct level "so that the situation doesn't become a problem, and a problem doesn't become a crisis." Indiana Secretary Todd Rokita similarly sends deputies or enters polling places himself to observe elections firsthand. Rokita was authorized to do so under a state law that allows the Indiana Secretary to enter polling places when that position is not on the ballot. And like Chapman, Rokita's office maintains a statewide voter helpline for election issues ranging from locating a polling place to reporting suspected vote fraud.

Secretaries Rokita and Handel both have pushed for greater protections in the absentee voting process. Rokita advocated for a bill that would penalize individuals who campaign in the presence of someone with an absentee ballot, in order to "be sure an absentee voter can vote in private without feeling pressured to vote for a candidate or party standing at her door while she completes her ballot."[16] And Handel pushed to make impersonating voters in the absentee ballot process a felony, just as it is when people impersonate voters on Election Day. To Handel, "Fraud is fraud. I don't care how it is conducted." And to Handel, it was important to increase the penalties for voter initiated election fraud in the absentee process as the number of voters voting absentee increased.

> "We needed to make sure we were looking at the [absentee voting] process and [address] its susceptibility to fraud, just as much as we were addressing in person voter fraud. It is just one step to ensure the overall integrity of the process. You don't want to deal with just in person [fraud], you have to deal with the entire process."

Collecting both quantitative and qualitative evidence on where fraud and deception exists within the system is crucial to ensuring that efforts to address such trickery are targeted appropriately. Maine Secretary Dunlap noted that many rumors of voters voting twice focus on students, but the evidence he's seen does not support such conjecture. "We've prosecuted one case of voter fraud in my time," Dunlap recalled.

> "It wasn't a college student, it was a bank vice president. The guy had moved from Lincolnville, Maine. Before he left Lincolnville he voted absentee. And then he meets this lady, they become friendly, she's running for school board, he wants to vote for her, so he registers again [in his new town] and he votes [on Election Day]. And of course these clerks talk to each other. And [one clerk asked another to check and see if he had voted before he left Lincolnville] and sure enough he had."

16 *Tackling Fraud with Voter ID and Absentee Reform*, Indiana Secretary of State, March 30, 2005, available at: http://www.in.gov/sos/securities/3123.htm (accessed July 28, 2009).

Beyond collecting and responding to qualitative evidence of trickery in the democratic process, other Secretaries have worked to develop data driven analyses to determine where fraud does exist in elections. Mississippi Secretary Delbert Hosemann, for example, published a report following two special elections in 2008. At the request of Mississippi state Judge Jim Parsons, Hosemann's office placed representatives in nine precincts throughout the county that was holding the special election. What Hosemann's team found, he said afterwards, was a "well-oiled machine" that "apparently had been run before." Hosemann's report documented several candidates and representatives of a campaign assisting voters "whether they needed it or not" and estimated that 50 to 75 percent of all voters in the county received such "assistance." Under Mississippi state law and Section 208 of the Voting Rights Act, Hosemann's report noted, "only the disabled, blind or illiterate can receive assistance, and then only when they ask for it." Thus campaigns offering to assist voters who do not need assistance and did not ask for assistance were violating the law and potentially bullying voters into voting a certain way. Secretary Hosemann did not have the legal authority to do anything other than collect the data, however, and the report was passed on to the Attorney General's office and the U.S. Attorney's Office.

That same year, Connecticut Secretary Susan Bysiewicz also developed a plan to collect data and evidence of deceased citizens who'd been counted as having voted in recent elections. Upon launching the investigation, Bysiewicz noted that a "journalism class found that hundreds of dead voters cast ballots in recent elections. As we prepare for our national election it is absolutely critical that we have clean, accurate voter lists," she noted. "Sloppy lists will not be tolerated."[17] In Connecticut, local clerks are required under state law to inform local voter registrars of deaths in their area to help with updating voter lists.

By collecting evidence on where problems exist in the elections process, Secretaries are more apt to make informed decisions on how to best address and enforce election law. This could involve developing enforcement strategies similar to Chapman's and Handel's. And it can entail promoting education of where the problems exist so that voters, candidates, and elections officials are informed on the parameters of the law and equipped with information on how to comply and to stop violations they observe.

The Secretary Enforcing Campaign Finance Regulations

Finally, many Secretaries are charged not just with enforcing the law to protect voters and the process, their office can also serve as a clearinghouse for reporting campaign contributions and expenditures, and recommending prosecution of any

17 Shomial Ahmad, *Bysiewicz Launches Investigation into Dead Voters*, Connecticut Public Broadcasting Network, available at: http://www.cpbn.org/bysiewicz-launches-investigation-dead-voters (accessed July 28, 2009).

violations. But most who claim this responsibility, however, are only required to respond to third party requests for audits and complaints. For example, the Nevada Secretary of State's office is required to provide all campaign finance reports within thirty days of receipt. The office will issue a warning letter if a candidate or committee does not turn in required forms, but according to an election official in the office, they "only initiate complaints when they are brought to our attention."[18] If any violations give ground to a civil suit, the Secretary of State refers the information to the state Attorney General's office. One election official estimated that "in any given election cycle, the Nevada Elections Division of the Secretary of State's office refers between sixty and eighty such matters."[19]

Within statutory guidelines, some Secretaries have sought to promote innovative and efficient methods of tracking and reporting campaign finance information. When former West Virginia Secretary Betty Ireland took office, she made it a priority to update her state's campaign finance reporting system. Knowing that posting scanned reports on her website would only be partially informative because they were not searchable, Ireland asked the state legislature to require all candidates for statewide office to file electronically. "In doing so," she recalled, "that makes every one of their pages instantly accessible and searchable." This "of course gives us transparency and that's exactly what we're looking for." Ireland was able to use her role as Secretary not just to enforce that law, but to advocate for its passage.

And in Oregon, the Secretary of State is empowered to impose administrative penalties to enforce campaign finance violations. Though Oregon law provides for penalties of up to $10,000 for such offenses, Secretary Bradbury created a Penalty Matrix to establish a fair and transparent method of evaluating violations and instituting penalties. The Matrix recommends graduated penalties that vary depending on the entity's prior offense or level of inaccuracies in their report. For example: "the penalty for any missing or insufficient item in a report except those regarding details of personal expenditures, a fine of $10 is assessed for a first offense, $15 for a second offense, and $20 for any additional offense. Failure to provide detail of a personal expenditure results in a penalty of 5% of the personal expenditure itself."[20]

Conclusion

While other officials in the state are charged with prosecuting offenders, a Secretary of State often has the responsibility to administer and interpret state and federal election law. This responsibility, and the vast amount of discretion

---

18 *Surveying the Landscape of State Campaign Finance Enforcement: A Preliminary Analysis*, 4 ELECTLJ 329 (2005).

19 *Id.*

20 *Id.*

that accompanies it, means that Secretaries have a great deal of ability to ensure that the laws are enforced in a way that protects voters' access to the democratic process and ensures that election results are accurate reflections of the public's will.

Thus it is not only important that Secretaries take this responsibility seriously, but that they actively work to ensure the enforcement of election law and protections throughout their state. This means embracing their role to ensure the statewide voter file is accurate. It means working with state and local law enforcement authorities, as Washington Secretary Sam Reed did to investigate the submission of false and duplicate voter registration forms, to ensure they are prioritizing the prosecution of election law violations. And it entails working with voters, candidates, and other actors in the political system to ensure that they know and follow the law.

In the absence of such leadership, enforcing election law is left to the whim of federal, state, or local prosecutors who may, or may not, place such enforcement at the top of their priority list. But if Secretaries work with those prosecutors, leading or encouraging investigations into possible violations of election and campaign finance law, voters in their states can rest easy under the assurance that the democratic process is protected.

Indiana Secretary of State
Todd Rokita

First Elected: 2002

In the view of Todd Rokita, "to find a quote unquote nonpartisan is to find someone in a bubble." And "this idea that you could have some nonpartisan appointed bureaucracy to be your state election official is a recipe for disaster." So long as Secretaries are elected by the voters of the state, he reasons, "the process at the end of the day is in the peoples' hands."

Rokita calls photo identification requirements for voters his "claim to fame." The fact that support for the requirements has generally fallen along partisan lines—with Republicans supporting and Democrats generally opposing the laws—surprised him. "I didn't expect it to be partisan," he noted, "but we're in this era of distrust. And this country is so divided. So any move you make it seems like you're making half the people angry." He arrived at the reform as a priority for his office because as he campaigned around the state among Republicans during the primary phase of his election "this was always on their mind." Their concern, he recalled, was "the idea that people are cheating." And to Rokita, requiring all voters to prove their identity with photo identification on Election Day "introduces a level of confidence for the voter." The requirements "build trust in the process."

And protecting that trust, Rokita says, is paramount to his work as the state's chief elections official. "It doesn't make headlines," he notes, "but there's a freedom fighter aspect to this. We are on the front lines of protecting an idea, and the idea is that the best way to run a society is when the people pick their own leaders." And Rokita's work is to preserve access while highlighting the need to institute safeguards against voter-initiated fraud. "So as much as I want everyone to participate and try to encourage that," he reasoned, "I get a lot of satisfaction in making sure that the process is defended and available." Improving turnout is important to Rokita, but balance is important as well. He explained, "if you don't measure all of that accessibility with measures of integrity then you're not going to get that balance. And you need it."

Chapter 10
The Secretary as Certifier: Recounts and Initiatives

> "For me, the unwobbling pivot upon which this whole process turns is that little old lady who casts her vote or affixes her signature to a petition. [T]hat's what I'm the guardian of. Never mind the agenda about whether or not something gets on the ballot, or a candidate wins or loses. The public trust begins and ends with my role as the guardian of her vote and signature."
>
> Maine Secretary Matt Dunlap

When the role of the Secretary of State was propelled into the spotlight with Florida Secretary Katherine Harris in the 2000 presidential election, it came with the headline: Recount. To many, Harris's oversight of the statewide recount of votes for president, and her ultimate certification of the results, solidified her role as a significant figure in determining the outcome of the presidential election.

Certifying the results of an election or reviewing signatures to certify the placement of a candidate or initiative on the ballot is one of the most influential aspects of a Secretary of State's duties. The role is born out of the Secretary's general responsibility as the state's record keeper. Just as many Secretaries are charged with keeping and protecting official documents and reports for their state, they are expected to oversee and finalize the counting of signatures and votes in support of candidates and ballot initiatives. But this important role of a Secretary of State operates in one of two ways: it is either completely overlooked or thrust into the spotlight.

The spotlight shines brightest when it becomes clear that the results of an election will hang in the balance of Secretaries' decisions. And it shines brighter when the results of the election carry national implications. For example, while there were several local and statewide recounts in the cycles following the 2000 election, none captured more headlines than those overseen by Secretary Sam Reed in Washington and Secretary Mark Ritchie in Minnesota. And both Reed and Ritchie instituted a careful and evenhanded recount process that, unlike the Harris recount in 2000, were free of any significant or credible allegations of partisanship.

Apart from recounts, a related role that garners less attention but that has similar potential for controversy is Secretaries' responsibility to certify, or approve, the signatures collected in support of candidate and initiative petitions. Nevada Secretary Ross Miller noted that in his state the initiative process is where "a lot of the battleground is taking place." "We're seeing so many initiatives," Miller noted, "and so many of them are high stakes policy matters."

And as with recounts, Secretaries have a key discretionary role to play in overseeing the validation of the signatures that are collected in support of initiatives and candidates. And decisions made under that discretion may not always make headlines, but have significant effects in determining what, or whom, gets on the ballot.

The Secretary as Certifier of Petition Signatures for Candidates or Initiatives

Maine Secretary Matt Dunlap has worked throughout his tenure to ensure that he reviews and certifies petitions in a fair and evenhanded manner, even if his own political party sues him as a result. To Dunlap, "I'm a Democrat but my viewpoint is that the way that I best serve the interests of my party is to do the right thing, regardless of what their temporal desires are to get someone off a ballot or stop an initiative in its tracks."

Dunlap was challenged to put his principles into practice when he was faced with a decision of whether a conservative ballot initiative referred to as the "Taxpayer's Bill of Rights," or TABOR, had properly submitted sufficient signatures to get onto the ballot.[1] Maine law requires that groups or individuals gathering signatures for petitions have one year from the date they receive their petitions to submit their collected signatures. Thus, when the group collecting signatures from TABOR picked up their petitions from the Maine Secretary of State office on October 21, 2003, they were subsequently required to return the petitions with collected signatures by October 21, 2004. "And that is specifically what happened with the TABOR initiative," Dunlap explained. On the day when they were required to submit their signatures, he recalled, the group held "a big press conference. They bring them in and they drop them off, and off they go to celebrate. And then someone feels something under their seat. And it's a big bundle of [signed] petitions they forgot to bring in. So they come in at 8:00am the next morning [to drop off the remaining petitions] and [they] said 'we forgot these.'"

It was Dunlap's first month on the job. He asked the head of the state Bureau of Elections, to keep the late petitions separate. But a few days later he received a call from the chief of the Bureau letting him know that the late petitions "made a difference. If we don't count them, they don't get [on the ballot]." Dunlap recalls:

> "We were torn, because there was this statutory provision that said 'one year,' and then you have the broader constitutional issues about the right to petition government. We really kicked it around and we knew that we were doing something very very politically dangerous for an administrator. We took a run at the law and we accepted the signatures."

---

1 The "Taxpayer Bill of Rights" or TABOR initiative in Maine was one of several proposed in states throughout the country. It generally required that any tax increase beyond basic increases for inflation be approved by a majority of voters in the state via referendum.

As a result of Dunlap's decision to accept the late signatures, the initiative, which Republicans generally supported and Democrats generally opposed, would get onto the ballot.

Dunlap, a Democrat, sought to make a pragmatic decision based on the principle that the law should be interpreted to allow for the validation of as many signatures as possible. But he recalled how difficult it was to implement a neutral decision with clear implications for both political parties. "There were people [within the Maine Democratic party] who wouldn't speak to me. I had a number of members of leadership openly talking about how we needed a new Secretary of State. And I got sued. [The state Democratic Party] said I had broken the law" by accepting the signatures. Dunlap's team argued in response that he "had the discretion to make the decision," and emphasized that it was a nonpartisan, "bureaucratic administrative decision." They argued that the 50,000 signatures were submitted "five business minutes late" and to "dismiss them … didn't pass the public straight face test, the intent of the law."

Dunlap took the case all the way to the Maine Supreme Court.[2] The Court upheld Dunlap's decision and struck down the law as unconstitutional, finding that it placed too great a burden on petition circulators. The court particularly found an implicit constitutional right of the circulator to choose when to file the petition, noting that the law "denies initiative proponents the reasonable flexibility allowed by the Constitution to circulate their petitions, to choose a filing date, and to file up to the dates set out in article IV, part third, section 18."

To Dunlap, his decision to accept the signatures was not "particularly courageous." It was simply "the right thing to do," even if it ultimately placed a Republican-supported ballot initiative on the ballot. "A lot of the Democrats didn't want this on the ballot," Dunlap recalled, "out of a fear that its presence on the ballot would energize Republican voters to turn out to vote for the proposal."

Maine voters later rejected the initiative. Dunlap observed that its presence on the ballot ended up "energizing the progressive left" to turn out to defeat it, leading one Democratic State Senator in Maine to declare Dunlap a "political genius." Dunlap thought "that was a stretch," but saw the entire experience, the first major controversy of his tenure, as an "example of the [partisan] vortex that you are thrown into" even though he was focused on issuing "what seemed to be a clear rendition of the law."

Dunlap's view on certifying signatures and his experiences of the implication of his decision in dealing with the TABOR petition foreshadowed his later decision in reviewing signatures for a candidate petition for Herbert Hoffman.

Hoffman ran as an independent candidate for the United States Senate in 2008. Maine law required Hoffman to collect 4,000 signatures in order to be placed on the 2008 election ballot. Hoffman submitted 4,112 signatures. John Knutson, the chairman of the Maine Democratic Party, challenged the validity of multiple signatures and whole petitions, claiming that signatures were improperly collected.

2 See *McGee v. Dunlap*, 2006 WL 1670283 (2006 Me.Super).

He argued specifically that some of the signatures were made outside of Hoffman's presence. Under a strict reading of Maine election law,[3] this made them invalid.

In response to the challenge, Dunlap invalidated three signatures on the grounds that the circulator was not present or otherwise aware that the signer was signing the petition, and ultimately invalidated seventy-four signatures for various reasons. 4,038 valid signatures remained, enough to place Hoffman on the ballot.

Knutson appealed Dunlap's determination to Superior Court claiming that three entire petitions (the petitions on which the three signatures were invalidated in the initial challenge) should be invalidated because the oath that Hoffman, as circulator, signed declared that all of the signatures on the petition were made in his presence. As at least one of the signatures from each petition was made outside of Hoffman's presence the oath was not valid and therefore, Knutson argued, the entire petition should be invalidated. Dunlap argued in court that the signatures should be accepted, emphasizing his discretion under the statute to accept or deny the entire petition when some of the signatures were not given in Hoffman's presence. The trial court agreed with Dunlap, but the State Supreme Court ultimately disagreed. "Although the Secretary's policy decision, attempting to save petitions in certain circumstances, may not be unreasonable," the court held, the "plain language of the statute must be effectuated."[4]

Beyond the mere reviewing of signatures for their validity under state law, Secretaries are also uniquely positioned to protect voters from fraudulent activity in the signature gathering process. In 2008, Oklahoma Secretary Susan Savage submitted a report to the Oklahoma Supreme Court citing numerous irregularities and potentially fraudulent signatures in Ward Connerly's effort to amend the Oklahoma constitution to ban affirmative action. And while Oklahoma law does not give Savage the authority or discretion to disqualify signatures that appear to be fraudulent, it did compel the Secretary to give any details as to the fraudulent nature surrounding any of the signatures.

But state law did require Savage to submit a report to the Oklahoma Supreme Court regarding the number of signatures counted, leaving it to the Court to determine whether the signatures were numerically significant. Savage's report advised the Oklahoma Supreme Court that the petition's signatures were rife with irregularities, and her office took great effort to carefully document these inaccuracies. In part, the report noted that a count of the signatures "has resulted in an unprecedented situation where large numbers of duplicate names and addresses were discovered well into the signature counting process."

After submission to the Supreme Court, Oklahoma law required that the Secretary publish a notice that the initiative is approved, preceding a period

3 Me. Rev. Stat. tit. 21-A, § 354(9).

4 *Knutson v. Dep't of Sec'y of State*, 954 A.2d 1054, 1062 (Me.2008). Hoffman then filed an action for preliminary injunction and TRO in federal court, seeking to have Hoffman's name placed on the ballot but both motions were denied. *Hoffman v. Sec'y of State of Maine*, 574 F.Supp.2d 179 (D.Me.2008).

within which a citizen of Oklahoma may file a protest. The ACLU and NAACP subsequently filed an objection to the signature count, based upon the findings in Savage's report.[5] Among their allegations were the charges that the initiative was "misleadingly and deceptively circulated." A few weeks later, Connerly's group withdrew the petition.

Secretary Savage's findings echoed those raised in Michigan when an identical initiative was up for consideration there a few years prior. In 2006, a federal district court found that there was "widespread fraud" that plagued the signature collection efforts for an identical petition from Connerly in her state. Between June and December 2005, several individuals circulated petitions, dubbed "MCRI", or the "Michigan Civil Rights Initiative" to place Connerly's proposal to ban affirmative action in Michigan on the November 2006 ballot.[6] During that time period, the court later found, the circulators engaged in a pattern of fraud that involved deceiving voters into believing that the petition supported affirmative action when, in reality, it would ban the practice.[7] A subsequent investigation from the Michigan Civil Rights Commission collected over five hundred affidavits from citizens who were either personally victims of "fraud and deceit" or who "offered anecdotal or observational testimony about friends and/or relatives who signed the MCRI petition under the belief that they were signing a petition to support affirmative action."[8] One witness testified in federal court that a circulator approached her in a shopping center, asking her "if she supported affirmative action." When she said that she did, the circulator asked her to support a petition to keep affirmative action alive by helping to put the MCRI on the ballot. When the witness asked to see the back of the petition to read the text of the initiative, she was shown only a "script" that the circulator had attached to the back of his clipboard. The script instructed circulators to ask registered voters: "'Do you believe in affirmative action? If so we need to work together to save it by putting it on the ballot in November. Please help keep affirmative action alive. We need you to sign now.'"[9]

---

5 *Objection to the Signature Count and Protest to the Initiative Petition*, In re: Initiative Petition No. 387, State Question No. 737, (Okla. 2008), http://www.aclu.org/images/asset_upload_file678_34595.pdf (accessed March 1, 2009).

6 Michigan state law gives petition circulators 180 days to collect signatures. Mich. Comp. Laws §§ 168.472a (2007). The petitions were delivered to the Secretary of State's office for review in January 2005, at the end of that 180-day, or six month, period. See generally Terri Lynn Land, *Michigan Secretary of State, Staff Review of Initiative Petition* (2005), available at: http://www.michigancivilrights.org/media/SOS-MCRI-Staff-Report7132005.pdf [hereinafter SOS Review].

7 *Operation King's Dream*, 2006 U.S. Dist. LEXIS 61323, at *33–35.

8 *Id.* ("This group also consisted of citizens who were approached by circulators, but who did not personally sign the petition because they were previously aware of its true purpose or because they read the petition and understood it to be an anti-affirmative action petition"). See *id.* at *16–25.

9 *Id.* at *23.

Upon receiving the petitions and signatures, Secretary Land's office reviewed a random sampling of the petition signatures, examining 500 of the approximately 508,000 signatures filed.[10] At question was the determination of whether there was a sufficient number of valid signatures to place the initiative on the ballot. At least 203 signatures of the sample would need to be invalidated in order to meet the numerical threshold required to render the entire signature collection insufficient.[11]

Secretary Land's office concluded that only fifty of the 500 signatures were invalid.[12] Subsequent challenges from a nonprofit organization claimed that 325 of the signatures in the sample were either facially invalid or garnered by canvassers misrepresenting the petition. Reviewing those challenges, and rejecting a sizable number, Secretary Land submitted a report to the state Board of Canvassers that concluded that the petition was supported by an adequate number of valid signatures.[13]

Both Savage and Land's discretionary decisions illustrate the effect that those decisions can play in addressing allegations or suspicions of fraud in the signature collection process. Savage's decisions to investigate allegations of fraud led in part to the ultimate withdrawal of the initiative. In Land's case, a federal court later concluded that the petition circulators had "engaged in systematic voter fraud," and suggested that Land should have further investigated allegations of fraud in the signature gathering process.[14] In both cases, Secretaries wielded significant influence over the ultimate decision of how to best respond to the allegations of fraud.

---

10 Michigan law required at least 317,757 signatures to get the petition on the ballot. *Id.* at *7.

11 SOS Review, *supra* note 6, at 2 (noting that in addition to the fifty invalid signatures already confirmed by the Secretary of State as facially invalid, "[a]t least 153 of the … challenges would have to be accepted [as fraudulently gathered] to render the petition insufficient").

12 The sample would have to reveal that the number of valid signatures was 297 or less in order to be insufficient. SOS Review, *supra* note 6, at 2; see also *Operation King's Dream*, 2006 U.S. Dist. LEXIS 61323, at *7 ("Under state law, the Secretary of State was not obligated to go beyond performing these ministerial functions in approving the petition").

13 SOS Review, *supra* note 6, at 2; see also *Mich. Civil Rights Initiative v. Bd. of State Canvassers*, 708 N.W.2d 139, 142 (Mich. Ct. App. 2005) ("On July 13, 2005, the staff review report was issued, which examined the 500 sampled signatures, and found 450 valid signatures and 50 invalid signatures … The report further concluded that the petition was sufficient under the standard procedures traditionally employed to sample petitions").

14 *Operation King's Dream*, 2006 U.S. Dist. LEXIS 61323, at *5.

The Secretary as Certifier of Election Results

As in decisions over validating signatures for initiatives and candidates, most Secretaries' certification of votes cast in an election provides little reason for fanfare. But in the handful of times when elections are close, their role as the state's certifier of election results positions them as an overseer of a recount. And it is in their role as director of those statewide recounts that many Secretaries have found themselves under increased scrutiny.

Idaho Secretary Ben Ysursa has worked to always "take the route that the laws are to be enforced in a fair manner." In 1984, Ysursa, a Republican, dealt with the presumptions and questions of whether he was conducting an evenhanded recount. That year, he recalled, the recount was for a congressional election in a heavily Republican district, in which just 170 votes separated the losing Republican incumbent and his winning Democratic opponent. After the Democrat was declared the winner, the Republican asked Ysursa's office to conduct a recount. "People from Washington [D.C.] thought there'd be some skullduggery with the Republican office holders trying to get their way back in," with the help of a Republican Secretary of State Ysursa recalled.

> "And so we went around and of course opened up ballot boxes and conducted the recount and the Democrat staffers called their bosses back in DC and they said there's nothing going on here. It was December in Idaho, which is a little wintry and they packed up their bags and left. A little before it ended. Everything was going fine."

Ysursa's recollection is typical of many Secretaries' intentions in conducting recounts: they seek to conduct them with a fair, even hand under the most intense scrutiny from both sides.

It is a level of scrutiny that Maine Secretary Dunlap found to be the most unexpected aspect of his job as Secretary. "You do these recounts and you can cut the air with a knife," he noted. "Rooms full of lawyers, the candidates not knowing where they're going to come down, one vote margins, tie votes," and the most important element, Dunlap emphasized is that the Secretary and their staff "know the law" better than anyone else in the room.

Beyond the level of scrutiny and the importance of careful application of the law, recounts have another side to them that goes beyond their specific electoral contest. They bring to light lurking problems in a states' election administration system. For in the succinct words of New Hampshire Secretary Bill Gardner, "if you don't have the experiences with recounts you don't get to see the problems" that may be lurking in the states' current elections process. It was Gardner's experience overseeing a recount involving punch cards and hanging chads in the mid-1980s that led him to ban the use of punch cards—over a decade before they became a problem for Harris and Florida voters in the 2000 election.

"The last straw for me with the punch cards," Gardner remembered, "was doing a recount [in] a race for state representative." Gardner performed the recount in the presence of the two candidates,

> "and we had the big lights and I was looking at the punch cards. I'd look at it and they'd both look at it and I said if only one corner is punched out, I'm not going to count it. But if two corners are punched out, I am going to count it. And so we went through it. And some of them weren't punched at all. And I would rule on those and I just said [that] what is important is to be consistent. And it ends up, the person who wins won by 3 or 4 votes. He said after I said ok you're the winner, he said I don't want it. If this is how I'm going to be picked to win, I don't want to win this way."

"Now picture the scene," Gardner recollected,

> "The person who lost then has to try to convince [his former opponent, the winner] to take the result. He said 'We don't like this but this is the way it was done, [and] you should [accept the victory].' And I'm sitting here watching this and I said to them I hope I never sit here again."

The candidates accepted the results, but Gardner worked to abolish punch cards as a result of the frustrating recount. Most of the rest of the country wouldn't learn of the confusing elements of voting with punch cards until the same issues arose to determine the outcome of the presidential election in 2000.

In the weeks following that election, problems with punch card ballots became one of the central controversies surrounding the elusive attempts to determine the ultimate winner of Florida's electoral votes. Some ballots were "dented," others had "hanging chads," or holes that were partially punched through but not completely divorced from the entire ballot. Manual recounts of ballots by hand led many counties to submit revised or amended vote totals, some of which Florida Secretary Katherine Harris rejected.[15] As a result, many local election authorities suspended their recounts until a subsequent order from the Florida Supreme Court ordered them to continue. Yet the order overturning Harris's decision did not come soon enough, and ultimately there was not sufficient time to complete a full recount of the ballots.[16]

---

15 The Florida Supreme Court ultimately ruled that Harris' decision to reject the amended results was an abuse of discretion. *Palm Beach County Canvassing Bd. v. Harris*, 772 So.2d 1273 (Fla. 2000). In *PBCCB v. Harris*, the court concluded "based upon our perception of legislative intent, we have ruled that election returns must be accepted for filing unless it can clearly be determined that the late filing would prevent an election contest or the consideration of Florida's vote in a presidential election."

16 Although the canvassing boards resumed their recounts after a November 21, 2000 order from the Florida Supreme Court, valuable time was lost and the results of several

After Harris's high profile decisions cast doubts on the outcome of the Florida presidential election, subsequent election cycles led to even greater attention on the manner in which Secretaries conducted recounts. And two Secretaries in particular—Washington Secretary Sam Reed and Minnesota Secretary Mark Ritchie—found themselves thrust into the national spotlight when they were required to oversee statewide recounts in major elections in their respective states. Both made it a priority to move forward with meticulous transparency and attention to fairness, aware of how even the perception of impropriety could taint both candidates' and voters' confidence in the ultimate outcome.

Washington Secretary Sam Reed and the Gubernatorial Recount of 2004

In 2004, Washington Secretary Reed was charged with overseeing three separate statewide recounts in the state's gubernatorial election. Dino Rossi, the Republican candidate for Governor found himself in a tight race against his challenger Christine Gregoire, a Democrat. Secretary Reed, a Republican, worked scrupulously to ensure all recounts following the close election proceeded in a nonpartisan and transparent fashion.

Reed initially declared Dino Rossi the winner—by 261 votes.[17] But because absentee ballots only had to be postmarked by Election Day to be valid, the declaration came before all of the absentee ballots had been received. This was of particular concern because over 60 percent of the voters in the state's largest county, King County, cast absentee ballots. The small margin of victory triggered a mandatory statewide recount. After the recount, Rossi was once again victorious, though this time by only forty-two votes. He was officially declared the winner of the machine recount on November 29, 2004.

The Democratic Party then requested a second, manual recount, paying over $700,000 to cover additional costs.[18] Reed recalled: "We were dealing with a lot of tough decisions. And the Democrats were, of course, very angry at me, because their candidate was behind and they had expected her to win in a [landslide]."

---

recounts were not included in the final tabulation by Harris, who refused to extend the court ordered deadline of November 26, 2000, even though she had discretion to do so. See e.g. Appellate Brief of Al Gore, *Al Gore v. Katherine Harris et al.*, 2000 WL 33998558 (Fla. 2000) at 5 stating "[f]ollowing a legal opinion from the Secretary of State calling into question the validity of manual recounts in vote tabulation, the Palm Beach Board voted to suspend its manual recount."

17 Kenneth P. Vogel, *Election Mess Heads to Court*, The News Tribune, Dec. 8, 2004, at A1.

18 Andrew Garber, *Democrats Will Finance a Statewide Hand Recount*, The Seattle Times, Dec. 3, 2004.

Roughly a month after Election Day on December 6, Reed oversaw the beginning of a recount of almost three million ballots.[19] Reed issued a ruling from his office that the recount would include only the ballots that machines had already counted. He wanted to avoid the tendency of "going back and look[ing] again at all the absentee ballots that were mailed in late, that weren't signed, that had the wrong signature, [and that were cast by] people [who] weren't really eligible." But as it became clear that several ballots in King County may have been wrongly omitted from the original tally, the Washington State Democratic Central Committee sued Secretary Reed to force him to develop "uniform standards" requiring the newly discovered ballots to be fully canvassed and counted under "liberal standards."[20] The Washington Supreme Court ultimately rejected the Democrat's argument and supported Reed's position that he was not required in a recount to add ballots "previously rejected in this election."

Reed explained that one of the "exceptions" that he made to his initial ruling on the recount was that "if we discover a mistake being made by the county, the elections people, then we will count those ballots. If there were ballots that should've been counted but for some reason [county officials] made a mistake, they would be included." And initially, according to Reed, the Republican Party did not have a problem with that exception. Until, in Reed's view, "things started to shift. And the Republicans sued me, to stop the counting of wrongly rejected ballots and it went all the way to [the State] Supreme Court."

Subsequently, and with the support of Secretary Reed, the King County election board began recounting 573 ballots that were wrongfully omitted from the first counting because elections officials had inaccurately labeled them as having no signature. The Washington State Republican Party then sought a restraining order to block the counting of the previously uncounted ballots. The lower court granted the injunction, but Reed and the Democratic Committee successfully appealed and had the decision overturned. In *Republican Party v. Election Servs.*, 153 Wn.2d 220, 221 (Wash. 2004), the Washington Supreme Court found that certain ballots were wrongly coded as having "no signature on file" without having been fully examined to properly place them in that category. Keeping with its previous ruling that "ballots are to be 'retabulated' only if they have been previously counted or tallied," the court also acknowledged that "under proper circumstances a canvassing board may decide that ballots should be recanvassed before certification of a recount." The court also noted that the Secretary of State's Director of Elections, Nick Handy, had provided a "detailed declaration explaining how other counties have already counted votes from ballots not counted in the original returns for this election."

The court reversed the restraining order, allowing the counting of previously rejected ballots. "The Republicans were upset with me," Reed recalled, "and then of course when things really shifted and the Republicans started falling behind, [I

19 Vogel, *supra* note 17, at A1.

20 *McDonald v. Reed*, 153 Wn.2d 201, 202 (Wash. 2004).

heard about] it because I'm a Republican. Some of my own best supporters got really angry with me," he remembers, "but we had to do it right."

After the entire manual recount, with the additional ballots included, Reed announced that Gregoire was ahead by 129 votes and certified her as the winner of the election. Following the certification, Reed made a decision that was greatly unpopular with members of his own political party. Republican Gubernatorial candidate Rossi called for a new election and argued that the problems which plagued the November election created a "total mess" and "left voter confidence badly shaken."[21] Reed did not support or endorse Rossi's request on the grounds that there was no provision in Washington state law that provided for a new election or "revote."

Secretary Reed issued a final declaration on December 30 that Christine Gregoire was the elected Governor of the state of Washington. During her inauguration speech, she called for election reform and an election task force to be headed by Secretary Reed.[22] Following the inauguration Reed "proposed a huge sweeping package of election reforms," which included online voter registration, heightened voter identification requirements, and moving the date of the primary election at least four weeks earlier to provide additional time to prepare for the general election.[23]

Reed pointed to the 2004 recount saga as both the highlight and the lowlight of his time serving as Secretary of State. "The highlight," he explained, "was that unlike Florida [Secretary Katherine Harris], I had gone through many recounts [as county auditor], including two congressional recounts. So, when it came time for a recount I knew exactly what to do, and I made it a point that every step of the way to be very transparent." Reed held press conferences "that were supposed last to twenty or thirty minutes would go on for an hour and a half." Reed worked daily to devote a significant amount of time "explaining to the news media" his decision-making processes. "We ended up going through four court cases," Reed noted, but throughout it all "we really did stay above the fray, we did what was right, [and] we did it fair."

But the lowlight, to Reed, was that he "really thought that the counties were better prepared, [and] doing a better job than they were." Instead, he found that "there were mistakes made in about twenty counties. [And] when you start putting a magnifying glass and have that few votes" it is easier to see the cracks in the voting process. In particular because of the problems in King County, Reed said, "we ended up getting skewered."

21 Ralph Thomas, *Gregoire Declared Governor-Elect, but Rossi Wants New Vote*, The Seattle Times, Dec. 30, 2004.

22 Timothy Egan, *Questions Linger as Governor Takes Over in Washington*, New York Times, Jan. 13, 2005, at A20.

23 For a full review of Secretary Reed's proposed reforms, see Report from the Election Reform Task Force, March 1, 2005, available at: http://www.secstate.wa.gov/office/news_docs/ElectionTaskForceReport.pdf (accessed June 12, 2009).

But there was a silver lining. Reed was able to identify and propose changes to the way elections were run in Washington, including expanding his oversight authority to audit auditors' performance and funding the statewide voter registration database. Four years later, in 2008, Reed noted that the reforms were "already making a big difference," because of both his increased oversight of the process and ensuring that voters' confidence in the election system was restored.

Minnesota Secretary Mark Ritchie and the Senatorial Recount of 2008

In the weeks leading up to the 2008 election, Minnesota Secretary Mark Ritchie focused his offices' efforts on organizing voter registration drives, disseminating information about the upcoming election to maximize voter turnout, minimizing voter discrimination, and protecting the integrity of the election process. In September 2008, Ritchie declared that following an extensive voter outreach effort from his office, Minnesota set a new all-time voter registration record, 84 percent of eligible voters. Ritchie proudly declared that "Every indication is that Minnesota will reach the goal of 80 in 08, a turnout of 80 percent of eligible Minnesota voters."

"Setting a new record could only have occurred as the result of a wide-spread effort" Ritchie noted. Key components of the campaign included numerous partnerships with businesses and athletic teams who conducted over fifty voter registration drives over the summer of 2008. Ritchie also created a voter outreach website containing comprehensive, interactive information for citizens on the voting process.

Despite all of these strides, the headlines on Election Day a few months later nearly universally emphasized only one thing: the vote totals for the two candidates in the state's most high profile race, between incumbent Republican Senator Norm Coleman and his Democratic Challenger Al Franken differed by only a few hundred votes. After all localities submitted their results, Coleman led Franken by 221 votes—less than one half of 1 percent of the nearly three million ballots cast. Because Minnesota law required an automatic recount when the vote differential is under one half of 1 percent, Ritchie indicated soon after the election that a recount would follow but that his office would not rush the results. "No matter how fast people would like it," Ritchie said at the time, "the emphasis is on accuracy."

Almost immediately following the election, Ritchie convened a canvassing board under the guidelines of Article VII Section 8 of the Minnesota Constitution. The state constitution requires the Secretary of State to select two sitting state Supreme Court justices and two district court judges who are not up for reelection. In addition, Ritchie opted for hand recounts to be conducted in each county, as opposed to a central location, which he claimed would significantly reduce the cost of the recount. After the local recounts, the canvassing board would review any disputed votes.

One of the initial decisions of Ritchie's canvassing board came on November 26 when they denied a request from Franken's campaign to include about 12,000 absentee ballots in the recount that poll workers had initially rejected. But as in Washington State, after it became clear that over 1,000 ballots were wrongly rejected, the canvassing board issued a directive ordering all counties to review its pool of rejected absentee ballots and set aside any that had been wrongfully omitted from the final vote total.

One of the more notoriously omitted ballots belonged to Erick Garcia Luna, a prominent Democratic party activist who chaired the state party's Latino Caucus. Garcia Luna's ballot was properly signed and submitted, yet appeared to be rejected because an election official assumed his last name was Luna. When there was no Erick Luna found in the state voter file, the official rejected the ballot.[24]

Upon hearing anecdotal evidence like this, the canvassing board and Ritchie sent a notice to all local elections officials, asking them to re-examine all of the rejected ballots. The board specifically "expressed an interest in knowing the number of Absentee Ballots that may have been mistakenly rejected."[25] Coleman's campaign tried unsuccessfully to halt the counting of the rejected ballots via a lawsuit in Minnesota Supreme Court, arguing that Ritchie and the Canvassing Board provided "conflicting and unclear guidance" on determining that a ballot was wrongfully omitted from the count.[26] The Court rejected Coleman's petition, and ruled that if both the Franken and Coleman campaigns agree that a ballot was erroneously rejected, then it should be included in the recount.

Apart from the debate over counting improperly discarded absentee ballots, Ritchie also oversaw the canvassing board's review of a stack of challenged votes that had not been counted by the machines on election night. Under Minnesota law, the board was instructed to review the ballots where voters, for example, checked a bubble instead of filling it in. And where possible, the board was required to determine and record a voters' intent.[27] The board reviewed nearly 1,000 ballots and was able to issue unanimous decisions on interpreting the votes on all but fourteen of them.[28]

On January 6, 2009 the recount was complete. Through the addition of the rejected ballots and challenged votes, Franken had gained 225 votes and was

---

24 Joel Stein, *Franken v. Coleman: Still Counting in Minnesota*, Time Magazine, Dec. 13, 2008, available at: http://www.time.com/time/politics/article/0,8599,1866262,00.html.

25 Email from Deputy Secretary of State Jim Gelbmann, as quoted in the Minneapolis Star Tribune (Bob Von Sternberg, *Secretary of State's Office Asks Counties to Sort Rejected Absentee Ballots*, Dec 2. 2008).

26 *Coleman v. Minnesota State Canvassing Board*, 758 N.W.2d 44 (Minn. 2008).

27 Voter intent review is guided by Minnesota statute 204C.22.

28 *Minnesota Secretary on Minnesota U.S. Senate Recount*, Speech delivered to the 2009 National Association of Secretaries of State Winter Conference (Feb. 7, 2009), available at: http://www.c-span.org/Watch/Media/2009/02/07/HP/A/15198/MN+Sec+on+MN+US+Senate+Recount.aspx (accessed Aug. 23, 2009).

declared the winner. Coleman subsequently contested the results of the election, listing a wide range of problems that he alleged plagued the election and recount process. Though litigation and subsequent trials ensued, the ultimate results of the election remained unchanged.[29]

One month following the conclusion of the recount, Ritchie released his 2009 legislative agenda.[30] Its focus was on ensuring the state learned from any mistakes that led to the problems that emerged during the recount. The suggested reforms sought to "enhance three core areas of election administration: streamlining Minneosta's current voter registration process, simplifying absentee ballot voting, and improving the adminsitration of recounts." In announcing the proposed reforms, Ritchie declared, "I feel extremely fortunate to have inherited an elections system that is the gold standard for the nation … but there is always room to find ways to do it better." Ritchie emphasized that "Our experiences in the 2008 elections have shown us how good our system really is … and what areas require improvement."

Ritchie's reforms included allowing for online voter registration, allowing for early voting, centralizing and standardizing the uniform counting of absentee ballots, and reducing the vote margin that triggers an automatic, government-funded recount. But although the reforms passed the Minnesota legislature, Minnesota Governor Tim Pawlenty vetoed every one, calling them "partisan bills," because they failed to receive significant support from Republican legislators.[31]

Conclusion

In the initial weeks following the commencement of the Minnesota recount in 2008, Time Magazine surmised:

> What if the 2000 presidential election had hinged not on a diverse, messy, weird and slightly creepy hick state like Florida but on the most organized, practical and cordial one in the Union: Minnesota? What if, instead of going to court after court over hanging chads and butterfly ballots and whether a recount should happen, election officials had just calmly looked at each ballot and tried to figure out what the voter wanted?[32]

29 See, e.g., *Coleman v. Franken*, Ramsey County District Court (Case 62-CV-09-56).

30 *Secretary of State 2009 Legislative Agenda*, Minnesota Secretary of State, Feb. 11, 2009, available at: http://www.sos.state.mn.us/home/index.asp?page=10&recordid=329&returnurl=index.asp%3Fpage%3D10%26deptid%3D%26catid%3D%26mindate%3D01%2F01%2F2009%26maxdate%3D07%2F23%2F2009%26isarchive%3D0 (accessed June 12, 2009).

31 *Letter to Minnesota Senate President James Metzen*, Office of Governor Tim Pawlenty, May 22, 2009, available at: http://www.governor.state.mn.us/stellent/groups/public/documents/web_content/prod009549.pdf, (Governor Pawlenty's explanation for the veto), (accessed Aug. 23, 2009).

32 See, Stein *supra* note 24.

"That's exactly what's going on in Minnesota," the reporter noted. Ritchie's leadership and the management of his office resulted in the efficient coordination of the recount, the absence of any substantial partisan issues and the consistent unanimity of the canvassing board with regard to each challenged vote. However, his ability to protect voters' rights during the recount was limited to a general managerial role, and most of his actions involved a dedicated adherence to the letter of the law. And after the recount, Ritchie sought to lead efforts to reform the parts of the law he felt needed changing.

Ritchie's example, which mirrored Secretary Reed's emphasis on transparency in 2004, illustrates how Secretaries can best embrace and execute their role as "certifiers in chief." Whether making decisions about the validity of signatures or votes, Secretaries must, in the words of Nebraska Secretary John Gale, act "as a judge would … making written rulings of law and findings of fact." In doing so, they ensure that recounts or reviews of signatures collected for candidates or initiatives are reliable and respected.

This involves combining a scrupulous adherence to transparency, accuracy, and the law with a commitment to using any arising controversies as springboards to implementing improvements to their election system in their states. As an editorial in the Minneapolis Star Tribune noted towards the end of the Minnesota recount, Ritchie's transparency and dedication to getting the recount right "has made it more likely that when the end comes, it will be accepted as fair."[33]

33 Editorial, *Canvassing Board Inspires Confidence*, Minnesota Star Tribune, Dec. 29, 2008.

Washington Secretary of State
Sam Reed

First Elected: 2000

Being a Secretary of State, to Sam Reed, is about leadership: "Leadership," he explained, "in terms of the bully pulpit, and to inspire all election administrators in the state to go beyond the statutory requirements and do more voter outreach, connect with the people, and get more participation."

Reed's strong and steady leadership was on display in the weeks following the 2004 gubernatorial election, when he was in the position of overseeing a close recount between two candidates for Governor. "There were mistakes made in twenty counties," Reed recalled. "The problem is that [the vote] ended up forty-six ten thousandths of one percent difference." His recount experience involved him being sued by both political parties at different points in the saga. For Reed, a Republican, it was particularly difficult when, in his words, "the Republicans started falling behind" in the count.

The experience led Reed to champion reforms to simplify the elections process. But those reforms did not include removing the party label from a Secretary of State candidate. Making the position nonpartisan would in his view do little to ensure that the officials serving in the office act in an impartial fashion. "In my experience working with non-partisan city councilmen and non-partisan mayors," Reed explained, "some of them are the most partisan people I know." And were party affiliation completely removed from the Secretary of State's office, he reasoned, "you make the Secretary of State weaker in terms of being effective in the capital, because of the very partisan legislators and a partisan Governor."

Instead, in Reed's view, it is incumbent upon voters to hold their Secretaries, whether Democrat or Republican, accountable to acting in a fair and unbiased manner. And Reed is a leader among all of the Secretaries in acting in exactly that way, with his actions in the 2004 recount serving as an example to other Secretaries of State on how to oversee a close and high-profile recount in a fair and judicious manner.

Conclusion
Secretaries, and Voters, as the Guardians of Democracy

The central premise of this book is that Secretaries of State play a crucial, pivotal role in ensuring that democracy is accessible and the results of elections are accurate and reliable. And in furtherance of this role, they serve as educator to advocate, protector, enforcer, reformer to certifier. With all of these comes the vital responsibility of serving as fair and unbiased guardians of the elections process.

To the extent that Secretaries do serve as "guardians of democracy," as this book contends, their ability to guard the process is closely linked to their ability to act, in perception and in reality, as unbiased protectors of the entire process. Secretaries are at their best when they are beholden not to any one bias or party, but to the voters whom they serve.

To Vermont Secretary Deborah Markowitz, being beholden to the voters of her state involves recognizing the common values that the citizens in her state share. "One," she explained, "is to eliminate unnecessary bureaucracy that stands in the way of the exercise of the franchise. So with every rule we ask: why are we doing this and does it make sense?" The other "is that when in doubt you count the votes, when in doubt you let a person vote. So whenever there is a question we defer to the voter." Thus in Vermont, "if a person comes in and their name is not on the voter [registration] list, and the clerk looks and sees that they were taken off of the [registration] list, their name was purged from the [registration] list, the voter is able to sign an affidavit swearing they still live in town and they are put back on the check list and allowed to vote." Or, "if somebody comes in and says they believe that they were registered and there is no record of registration because we never received a form, then again the voter gets to sign an affidavit saying that they filled out a registration form by the particular deadline date here and we put them on the checklist and they get to vote."

Missouri Secretary Robin Carnahan similarly points to her principal goal as being to serve the voters by making the elections process "efficient and accessible" and one that earns the confidence of her citizens. To Carnahan this means in part making sure that a voter's experience on Election Day is positive. "My view," she explained, "is that people's confidence in the elections and in the results of the elections often comes from the personal experience they have in a polling place on Election Day." Thus she considers it her responsibility to make sure the polling place is set up properly, lines are short, the precinct is run well, and "if there's a problem they deal with it properly."

Carnahan also emphasized the importance of taking a balanced approach to election administration. This approach is central to ensuring the fair and equitable administration of elections, and is one that promotes both access to the vote while also protecting the integrity of the process and accuracy of the outcome.

"Ultimately everything that has to do with voting to me is sort of like two sides of the coin," she said.

> "On the one side of the coin is guaranteeing access to every legitimate voter, to ensure that [their] voice can be heard. The other side is to make sure that there's no monkey business, and that people who shouldn't be voting or people who attempt to perpetrate fraud on the system, can't do that. So they're equally important. We focus on both of those things."

And though it doesn't often make headlines, this focus on both promoting access to the process while protecting its integrity underscores the agendas of many modern Secretaries. Kansas Secretary Ron Thornburgh emphasized repeatedly during our interview that the "fundamental cornerstone" of his work administering elections involves striking a "balance between accessibility and security." To Thornburgh, "The job of elections is very simple: to make sure that every vote that deserves to be counted is counted, and that every citizen who has the right, has the opportunity to vote." And to him, ensuring that every voter has access to democracy while protecting the integrity of the process involves "making sure that voter registration is available at every single possible place that voter registration is [supposed to be] available" while guarding the security of the voter's ballots once received.

Thornburgh also discussed how many individual reform measures he chooses to promote are those that are singlehandedly able both to promote access and protect the accuracy of the voting process. He pointed to online voter registration as one of those reforms. Like Secretaries in Minnesota, Arizona, South Dakota, and Washington, Thornburgh saw the concept as something that could expand registration opportunities while ensuring that the registration list remained accurate.

Under Thornburgh's proposal, when a person obtains their driver's license, they can simply answer a query stating that they would also like to be registered to vote. That information is then transmitted electronically to the Secretary of State's office, as well as to the local clerks. In Thornburgh's view, this addresses "the biggest problem we have on election day, [which] is when someone shows up and says 'I've registered to vote,' and their name does not appear on the rolls." Often times, Thornburgh explained, a voter's name is not on the list because their paper registration card "got lost between the DMV and the Secretary of State's office." Allowing the electronic sign up and inclusion on the registration lists significantly reduces the potential for error or loss of registration.

Thornburgh also pointed to his innovative approach to providing for satellite voting, which enables voters to cast their correct ballots outside of their home precincts. He explained, "What we've done is, instead of the old concept of I live in one place, therefore I have to go to this particular polling place to cast a vote," under satellite voting, electronic voting machines are programmed with every ballot in the county. Thornburgh then works with local elections officials to "take that voting machine to a place where the public actually is, and the public can just show up at a shopping mall or at some gathering place, [and] any person at any precinct can cast a vote in the week prior to the election at that satellite location." He noted that this is particularly advantageous in smaller communities, where, for example, his office "shows up on the Friday before the election with a polling machine, [and] opens a polling place for them on Friday at their own normal polling place." Then "we can then take that machine to another place on another day, and we can use the machines at a variety of different polling places leading up to the election. So we're more efficient in how we use the technology for creating the accessibility for the voter. And the voter is being served better because you don't have to show up between 7am and 7pm, which are some pretty artificial brackets on when you should be allowed to vote."

But beyond the improved accessibility of satellite voting, Thornburgh believes this program also protects the integrity of the election through improving the security of the ballot. "The weakest link on election administration," he explains, "is when we turn loose of the ballot." But "by satellite voting, we're actually keeping the elections officials and the sworn election judges in charge of the elections process. And so we've created accessibility and a higher level of security simply by creating a new way of looking at what Election Day really means."

In addition to making efforts to administer elections with an even hand, promoting access while protecting the integrity of the process, the most effective Secretaries of State are those who also have a sincere, demonstrable commitment to protecting the sanctity of the democratic process. Witness South Dakota Secretary Chris Nelson. To Nelson, the most rewarding aspect of his job as Secretary of State is

> "knowing every day that we are the people that make democracy happen. And, you know when I train election officials, that's how I begin every presentation. We have a tremendous privilege, [and a] tremendous responsibility to make democracy happen, and that it doesn't get any better than that. And we're going to take it seriously and we're going to do it right. And that's the way we approach it."

Iowa Secretary Michael Mauro similarly points to his demonstrable commitment to protecting the democratic process as the reason he was able to successfully advocate for a multiple of groundbreaking reforms in his state, like Election Day Voter Registration. Mauro notes that when he

> "came into the office of secretary of state, … it was with the right intentions: to be Secretary of State. I came here with the right motive. I'm not here to toot my own horn. I was so successful in [getting reforms through] the legislature [because they knew that] I wanted to do the right thing for the election process."

And, like Thornburgh, to Mauro the "right thing" means making sure that the process is "open to as many people as possible while at the same time trying to provide voter integrity and security." Mauro emphasized, "I want people to participate, I want as many people to participate, I want to make it as easy as possible for them to do that at the same time trying to provide the security and integrity of the process."

But importantly, even with the best of intentions, and the highest commitment to serving voters, there is never a guarantee that elections will run perfectly, with every eligible voter able to cast their ballot and every ballot counted accurately and securely. As Pennsylvania Secretary Pedro Cortés noted, "People have the right to expect a perfect election." But, he cautioned, "it's just not realistic. We have 9,300 polling places, 25,000 machines, 50,000 poll workers, 8.3 million registered voters, and then you have thirteen hours of voting, where poll workers have to be there for at least fifteen."

Indiana Secretary Todd Rokita similarly referenced "30,000 poll workers in Indiana," who "by definition are going to make a mistake." The reason, he notes, is because

> "people run the election, not the machines. The machines are a simple tool. So let's say you have an electronic machine and the county clerk forgets to plug them in the night before to charge the battery. Let's say a tornado comes through Indiana, electricity goes out in several precincts. Because the battery wasn't charged, the machine goes dead. That's not a failure of a machine, that's a failure of the checklist that the clerk should have gone through the night before. And even more important than that, the question then becomes, was that poll worker trained to know to go to paper ballots at that time so that the election could go on uninterrupted."

Rokita's remarks similarly illustrated the unique position that Secretaries hold. They are the people central to the process, the leaders who are called on to guide the ships of democracy and protect and preserve voters' confidence that their ballots will be counted and the results of the elections will be accurate. Their significant role in overseeing a smooth election requires that they embody a sincere and steadfast commitment to ensuring that they use every aspect of their office to promote access and protect the integrity of elections. Secretaries are most effective at achieving those goals when they recognize their unique responsibility to avoid partisan and political pressures and pursue the types of honorable and creative approaches to their position highlighted in the foregoing pages.

That is the good news. As these pages illustrate, apart from the headlines of Florida in 2000 and Ohio in 2004, Secretaries across the country, from either political party, are embracing their various roles as administrators of democracy. And in doing so, many are mindful to develop fair and transparent approaches to their work.

But one of the most often repeated guiding principles for many Secretaries, particularly those who are directly elected to the offices in which they serve, is the importance of accountability. For while Secretaries of State may be our guardians of democracy, the voters are the centerpiece of the elections process. And nearly every Secretary I interviewed, regardless of their political background or affiliation, mentioned accountability to the voters who elected them as a guiding principle for their work. These State Secretaries of State bring a nonpartisan, "public-trust first" perspective and approach to running elections because, in their view, the voters who employ them expect nothing less.

It thus is worth closing with an emphasis on the fact that, just as Secretaries must work to serve the voters and citizens of their state, voters also have a responsibility to hold these statewide elections officials accountable to promoting those two sides of the same democracy coin that Carnahan references. Voters who wish to see elections that are accessible to all and produce accurate reflections of the people's will cannot overlook their important role in the process. In most states, voters hold the keys to ensuring their state's chief elections official oversees the elections process in a fair, transparent, and judicious matter. Just as it is crucial for these principles to guide our Secretaries, it is critical that voters support and work with Secretaries of State to ensure that their goals and principles are reflected by whoever occupies that office. And when those citizens are working in collaboration with Secretaries to ensure that they are promoting fair, accessible, and secure elections, we are all brought closer to seeing that elusive perfect execution of democracy.

Index